People wishing to heal themselves, their environment, or their bodies by seeking a Spiritual path often run into resistance from the more accepted medical and psychological communities. Yet if those same people turn to mainstream therapies, they frequently feel alienated from themselves and from their Spiritual ideals.

The same may be true for healing professionals. The word "metaphysics" brings feelings of fear and impotency to many psychotherapists, while more holistically oriented practitioners may judge mainstream therapies as useless.

Mutual mistrust, both between people of differing philosophies and between the different parts of ourselves, may, at times, run rampant. It is because of this lack of understanding and cooperation that I have written this text. Health comes in the perfect form, at the perfect time.

Seek and ye shall find.

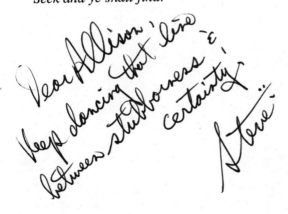

Healing Thoughts

*Applying Therapeutic Shamanism
In Your Daily Life*

Steven E. Rogat

© 2002, Steven Rogat
Creative Thought Press, Chapel Hill, NC, USA

This is a revised edition of *Healing Thoughts, Therapeutic Shamanism:
A Bridge Between Metaphysics & Psychotherapy*
©1997 Steven E. Rogat, Paintbrush Press, Parker, CO, USA

Healing Thoughts
   Applying Therapeutic Shamanism In Your Daily Life
      © 2002 Steven Rogat
      Creative Thought Press
      P.O. Box 2791
      Chapel Hill, NC, USA 27515

Revised Edition of:
   Healing Thoughts, Therapeutic Shamanism:
   A Bridge Between Metaphysics & Psychotherapy
   © 1997 Steven Rogat
   Paintbrush Press
   11844 N. Delbert Rd, Parker, Colorado, USA 80134
   Special Thanks to: Sandy & Andrew Welchel: Publishing Consultants

Cover Design by Nick Zelinger
   NZ GRAPHICS
   1445 South Quail Court
   Lakewood, Colorado, USA 80232

Special Thanks to Editorial Consultants:
   Marcia L. Rogat, Creative Thought Center
   Aysha Griffin
   803 Paseo De Don Carlos
   Santa Fe, NM, 87501, USA

Affirmation Dialogue chapter ©1997 by Steven Rogat

All rights reserved. No part of this book may be reproduced or used in any form or by any means - graphic, electronic, or mechanical, including photocopying, mimeographing, taping, or information storage and retrieval systems - without express permission from the author, except by a reviewer who wishes to quote brief passages related to a review written for inclusion in a magazine, newspaper, journal, or other broadcast. See *"About the Author"* at the end of the text to contact the author for more information.

Rogat, Steven E.
   Healing Thoughts
      Applying Therapeutic Shamanism In Your Daily Life
         Includes bibliographical references
International Standard Book Number (ISBN): 0-9672206-1-0
Library of Congress Catalog Card Number: 2002102424

Acknowledgments

I offer much thanks to my clients, friends and students who have helped me to learn and to teach. Without you, this book would not be here.

To my Dad, Saul, who by passing on decades ago, started me on my path. To my sister, Arline, who passed on before I had the pleasure of sharing this with her. To my Mom, Dorothy, and my brother, Larry, who just by being there, have given me another perspective. To my lovely wife, Marcia, having taught me patience and a belief in myself.

To my daughters, Emily and Brianna Fiola, for putting up with my ranting and raving. To my son, Joseph, who showed me that major interruptions are really minor side-trips in which I can enjoy myself.

To my many teachers in physical and Spiritual realities, too numerous to mention, who had faith in me even when I did not. Much love, shared healing, increased certainty, and THANKS!

The ripples DO go on forever!

The Stars, The Sky, The Earth Is Ours,
To Hold, To Mold, To Praise, And To Raise.

We Live In The Memory Of Our Own Future
And In The Growth And Healing Of Our Past.

We Are Shining And Growing, Loving And Living
And Dining On The Energies Within And Without.

The Light Of Spirit, The Warmth Of The Sun,
The Depths Of The Moon, Are Within The Grasp Of…

The Highest Of The High, And The Lowest Of The Low,
And We, Who Are What We Are,
Just Need To Reach Out…

And Touch The Hand Of The Creator.

Enjoy The Journey!

Table of Contents

Chapter 1. Changes...p.1
A personal path through dis-ease. Spiritual, physical, mental and emotional identity crises. Suspending beliefs & effecting healing.

Chapter 2. Kahuna Theory...p.5
Hawaiian Shamanism. A communications model. Comparative psychological models.

Chapter 3. The Soul's Journey.......................................p.13
The meaning of symbols. Higher & Lower Selves. Psyche & Eros, The Middleworld, Underworld & Overworld. Getting past the fear.

Chapter 4. The Psychic Accesses: Breathe & Relax Into Spirit
....p.21
Ordinary & non-ordinary reality. Thanatos, Narcos, Hypnos, Pythos, The yogic complete breath.

Chapter 5. Grounding...p.31
Spiritual & physical bodies. Personal mythology. Grounding vs. shielding. The adventurer vs. the warrior shaman.

Chapter 6. Asking for Guidance, Listening to Self..............p.47
The "Great Parent". White Light meditations - The Middleworld, Lowerworld & symbolism, The Upperworld & healing. The inner voice. Ideomotor responses & the pendulum. Self-response-ability.

Chapter 7. Prayer, Affirmation & Manifestation.................p.65
Beliefs & feelings.

Chapter 8. The Reality of Symbols..................................p.75
The environment as manifested symbols - journaling, meditation, dreamwork. Exploring & developing symbology & thoughts.

Chapter 9. Exploring the Past: The Challenge....................p.93
Conditioning & re-learning. Emotional thought clusters.

Chapter 10. The Body as Symbol................................p.105
Memories & symbols anchored within the body. Polarity therapy. Imagery & thought used for healing.

**Chapter 11. The Manifestation Process:
 Focus Clearly, Breathe Deeply, Believe Completely**..........p.119
Uncovering the resistance. Exercises to take out the "Kinks in the hose". Manifestation. An affirmation is alive!

Chapter 12. Affirmation Dialogue..................................p.131
True dialogue. Releasing the perfect resistance at the perfect time. Affirmations. Dealing with sadness & anger, "Burning Karma".

Chapter 13. Personal Power & Forgiveness......................p.145
The Power center. Abuse vs. use of power. Warrior vs. adventurer shaman. The white heart meditation. Past, present & future.

Chapter 14. Hear it, See It, Feel It, Heal It!......................p.157
Memories, healing & balance. "Gray Screen/White Screen" exercise. Generate the positive feelings. Remember the future & manifest!

Appendix I: Colors - Positive vs. limiting aspects

Appendix II: Numbers - Reducing to the lowest digit. The specific numbers: meanings, challenges & affirmations

Footnotes

Bibliography & Additional Reading

- - -

- 1 -

Changes

And being cast out of Heaven, incarnated in the body, separate from others and from Spirit...we search for the path that leads back Home.

There are many types of pop-psychology and self-help books on the market today, and an abundance of psychotherapeutic techniques in use. There are meditations, Spiritual paths, religious beliefs, individual feelings. We all wend our way through this maze of life, taking a little of this and a little of that, searching for the best route to take. This is a book about healing ourselves and our environment, a book about honoring ourselves as individuals rather than products of someone else's belief system.

We run into people that say this is right, and that is wrong. We cannot escape the preconceptions of right and wrong, enlightening and limiting. Dogmatically speaking, any belief system that excludes any and all other groups of beliefs may be limiting.

The best we can do is to experience something for ourselves, and decide whether that belief system is right or wrong for US.

We experience something, we try it on to see if it fits and holds truth for us. Hopefully we gain wisdom or insight from that. Yet, this process is in a continual state of change. We have different experiences all the time, and, therefore different conclusions. We need a guide in this journey of change, a map to help us recognize our thoughts, our feelings and our relationship with ourselves. In this way we encourage positive change and growth.

In this process we step back, observe ourselves, our experiences, our conclusions and actions. As we move beyond the past, we have the opportunity to create a more positive present and limitless future. We move beyond the person we had been a mere second ago. We are many people within this lifetime that we call "ours". Yet...

The one thing that remains present throughout the changes is the relationship we have with our selves.

This is beyond the mindless routine of merely being ourselves here and now. We become, by reviewing, evaluating and growing, more than just rats in a maze. We become builders of the maze itself. Getting in touch with the bigger picture - past, present and future - we identify more with the overseer of our lives. We become the overseer, with all of its creative potential!

Brief Overview of Author's Spiritual Quest

This text is based on my personal experience, first as a rat in the maze, and, gradually, as the builder. I've been through many different paths this lifetime. They have not been right or wrong. They just were, for each was right in its own time.

I had many shattering experiences as an adolescent and teenager. My identity crisis was coming on strong. I had no idea what I was doing on the Earth in the first place and no idea what to do while I was here. I was lost (I still am, but perceptibly it's a happier lost).

My first step in developing confidence, a positive self image and courage came at the age of sixteen when I learned about hope and the power of positive thought. Yet that was simply survival. Once I learned that I COULD survive, I dared to take the next step--deciding HOW to survive and be happy. Exploring my Spirituality, I got involved with Transcendental Meditation (TM) and the Hindu tradition. The experience definitely served its purpose--I enjoyed and celebrated life more. I was high. I made it. I was happy.

And then I got physically ill.

Around that time, I was planning on moving, separating from friends and family. There was pain, both physically and emotionally. I had the beginnings of lower back and sciatica nerve trouble, kidney problems, toxic headaches and a pronounced tendency toward having accidents. I was falling apart within. I strived toward getting higher and leaving my pain behind. I did get higher, but the pain persisted.

I moved cross-country and devoted myself to Kundalini Yoga for several months. I experienced more joy throughout my body. But the physical pain and the pain of separating from friends and family were still there. To get rid of that feeling of separation, I devoted my life to being of service to others. Being a workaholic, I got to ignore the pain, but it persisted. "OK," I thought, "time to address the symptoms through the medical profession." I went to doctors, then chiropractors, a psycho-therapist, acupressurist, nutritionist, Hathayoga teacher, and more. Each of these methods worked, temporarily. But the pain persisted.

Then came Tibetan Buddhism and Vipassana, sitting or "Insight" meditation. I experienced my pain as a construct of my mind, an illusion that I used to divert myself from the Spiritual path. I successfully found happiness amid the pain and separation experienced as a being apart from others on the Earth plane. I thought I'd finally found the trick to being HERE. But the pain persisted, and I was getting sick of being sick.

Becoming an Authority in My Life

By the time I was twenty-four, I had to sit and rest twice within a quarter-mile walk. I needed, once more, to explore healing options. I tried, what was to me, a last resort--a psychic or Spiritual healer. Learning of the body/mind connection, I worked with various types of breath therapy, regression, bodywork and Shamanic thought. I received help in releasing my mental and emotional tension, allowing the body to heal itself. I paid attention to, and gained cooperation from, my inner child and from Spirit. That is when my personal journey began!

I gave up much of my investment in the rules, beliefs, even feelings that I had adopted from others. I became personally involved with my own healing process. Letting go of limiting feelings and beliefs, I began to adopt more limitless ones. Yet, I found myself in a personal dilemma--though I couldn't completely accept all the philosophies thus studied, I was not willing to give them up either. So I started adopting what I could use from each of the philosophies. I found I was then able to complement, not reject, other belief systems such as Hinduism, Buddhism, Christianity or Judaism. Since my life was MINE, and *I* was response-able for the decisions I made in life, I used whatever philosophy and healing methods worked.

On a physical level, I went back to previously tried therapies. With the release of limiting thoughts and feelings, every technique became more effective. With my new-found freedom I was able to complement, instead of discount, my experience with doctors, chiropractors, acupressurists and others. My Spiritual path, my personal path, and my physical healing path all converged. I integrated many paths without discounting any of them. Some might argue that, had I given myself over totally to one path or another, I would have healed myself. However, that was decades ago, ancient history. It was not to be. Perhaps it was "destiny" that I learn to become the authority in my life, with a direct, personal relationship to my potential, my powerful, creative, loving healing source--Spirit.

I don't ask that you accept everything or anything within this text blindly. I still question it!

I ask that you consider it. Question it. See if it fits, if it holds truth for you. I will try to be accurate with the Spiritual and psychological models presented in this text. But, in the last analysis, you are viewing MY interpretation of various paths to healing and enlightenment. I may have no idea what I'm talking about, but I tell a really good story.

- - -

- 2 -

Kahuna Theory

...and a child shall lead them...

When attempting to empower ourselves with choices, we may find ourselves overwhelmed: How do we make the right choice and act on that? What are the consequences, the result of those actions? How do we learn from our mistakes and do better next time? These are all questions with which we've plagued ourselves at one point or another.

I have found it extremely useful to classify choices simply (there is plenty of time to make things complicated)--Is this goal, this thing I aspire to achieve, helpful, or is it limiting? What are the consequences? Do my choices help in increasing the life force and happiness of myself and all around me, or do they limit that life force and joy?

I include within this choice between helpful or limiting, not only myself but "all around me". We are not in this life alone! We have relationships with ourselves, others, the environment, people, animals, plants, the Earth itself. We are connected to EVERYTHING. Thoughts, feelings, reactions, interactions ALL abound. The Sioux have a wonderful phrase for this, "Mitakuye Oyasin" (mitakwe-assin), "All My Relations", that which encompasses everything. Putting life in these terms, we DO have relationships with everything around us. And we are response-able for the role we play within those relationships.

Yet, we are the ones who define the terms of our relationships. Only by first acknowledging the relationship we have with ourselves, with our own thoughts and actions, can we then expand our viewpoint "outward". What we think about our environment, how we respond to it, how we perceive it in the first place, is on an individual basis. That makes each individual's relationship with everything unique.

Everybody perceives things differently than everyone else. Therefore we cannot separate ourselves from our environment. It is part of us. We are part of it. Mitakuye Oyasin!

Healer of Relationships

Of the various definitions of a Shaman, I like Serge Kahili King's the best because it assigns life to, and respect for, those things we are in relationship with. We are acted upon, act on, and interact with everything within us and around us. King defines a Shaman as a "healer of relationships--between mind and body, between people, between people and circumstances, between humans and nature, between nature and Spirit."[1] The experts or master practitioners of this philosophy are called "Kahuna" in Hawaiian.[2]

Kahuna is a Shamanic belief system "originating" in Hawaii that teaches of a direct, personal relationship with Spirit. A Hawaiian word, Ka, in this context means "the". Huna means "secret" or "hidden knowledge"[3] and refers to the make up of personality. Its teachings include how to deal with different parts of ourselves, gain a better understanding of our world, facilitate healing and create a better reality for ourselves and those around us. In one way or another we are all on the path to becoming Kahuna. Sandra Ingerman, author of *Soul Retrieval, Mending the Fragmented Self*, expands this idea by stating, the "Shaman calls on Spirit to intervene on behalf of people"[4] in matters of importance on the Spiritual and Earthly planes.

The Shaman keeps an ongoing relationship with the world of Spirit. In other words, we have a daily relationship with our thoughts and our interactions with ourselves and everything around us. Defining this relationship is of utmost importance–it overshadows everything we do and, consequently, everything that happens within our lives.

Thought Is Creative

When defining this relationship, I recall the phrase drummed into my head, "Thought Is Creative!" Our thoughts not only effect our environment, but they create it as well. If my perceptions of everything differ from everyone else's, is this not so? If I respond to people uniquely, do they not respond to me uniquely as well?

"Thought is creative." This is a simple statement, yet one with many ramifications, one that requires explanation. Any rules that we come up with to explain how this applies to our lives are merely rules that WE have created. And to explore this concept, to understand, experience and apply it, we need to invent some parameters within which to work.

Lono - Ku - Kane
Middle Self - Lower Self - Higher Self

According to Kahuna lore we have three different parts of our psyche communicating and cooperating with each other, coexisting side by side. King refers to these three aspects of consciousness as "lono" (the mind or conscious mind), "ku" (the heart, body or subconscious), and "kane" (the Spirit or superconscious)[5]. Maxwell Freedom Long, an author and classic researcher of Huna lore, terms these parts of ourselves the Middle Self, the Lower or Basic Self, and the Higher Self.[6]

The Middle Self contains the mind and intellectual, logical aspects, while the Lower Self encompasses the body, memories and feelings or emotional aspects. The third part of the triune, the Higher Self, relates to Spirit, the Creative Self, and is considered the greater authority or overseer of the other selves. The thoughts and goals of the Middle Self combine with the feelings, thoughts and memories of the Lower Self to be manifested by the Higher Self. The interactions among the three selves define how our thoughts create our reality.

For simplicity purposes, the three selves can be considered as separate, although they are not, in actuality, separate at all. They are aspects of the whole person, yet they all work from differing states of awareness. Having different perceptions and energies, each has its own rules of governing behavior and thought. Another Hawaiian word, "Kanaloa", refers to the ideal integration of these three selves: the perfect interaction and cooperation between our various aspects. The challenge is to explore and improve these interactions in order to create a better reality for ourselves and everything around us.

A Communication Model

The interaction among the three selves in the Kahuna model can be likened to a more modern approach--Transactional Analysis (TA), originally developed by Eric Berne. Predominantly a communication model, TA refers to the three selves as the Parent (Middle Self) with its shoulds and don'ts, the Child (Lower Self) with its feelings and impulses, and the adult (Higher Self) with its objectivity and its ability to balance the other selves. I have found it helpful to refer to the Higher Self as the "shouldless parent", guiding the other selves with Love and objectivity. This is done without the judgments, limitations and shoulds that come to mind sometimes when thinking of parenting.

Although King does not liken "Ku", the Lower Self, to a child, it is understandable why Long does. Because the Lower Self is mainly concerned with memories, habits and learned emotional responses, it may simply be easier to treat the Lower Self as you might a child. In this way we can deal with those old habits and patterns, encouraging ourselves with love and respect...gently, yet firmly, as we would wish to do when dealing with a child.

The TA model calls for conscious interaction and communication among the three selves, allowing ourselves the chance to live a happy and more fruitful life. However, according to Long, as well as Enid Hoffman, another student and author of Huna lore, there may not be any direct lines of communication between the Middle (parent) and Higher (adult) Selves. The Higher Self can reach the Middle Self only through the Lower Self. We can reach our Higher Self only through our Lower Self.[7] Perhaps this is why some religious believers consider the Superconscious to be the "deepest" subconscious.

King feels, however, that this is not necessarily so. We can have direct contact between the Middle and Higher Selves, yet it is important to include ALL aspects of the self when facilitating healing. In actuality, I do not even know if it IS possible to ignore the Lower Self. Since this aspect of ourselves contains our habits, emotions, thoughts, feelings and MEMORIES of the past, the Lower Self is ALWAYS involved when perceiving and interacting with anything and everything.

I have seen many people deal with Spirit, with the Higher Self, while trying to ignore the Lower Self. The result is often an intellectual exercise that denies one's feelings and emotional needs. The reverse is true as well. Within various psychotherapeutic models, we may deal with the Lower Self, while trying to ignore the Higher Self, the Creative Force. Either division may lead to ignorance, unfulfillment and limitations.

Because of this, I encourage communicating through the Lower Self in all interactions between the conscious mind and Spirit. This way, we will not get into the habit of ignoring the "child self". Additionally, we do not wish to merely communicate between the Middle and Lower Selves without the recognition of, and Guidance from, the Higher Self. We can ask Spirit, the shouldless and limitless parent, for input whenever possible (that means "whenever we remember"). By including all aspects of consciousness, we remove any limitations before we have a chance to create them. We constantly affirm Kanaloa, the totality of Self, the integration of the three selves.

Psychoanalytic Theory

In another approach, we look at Freud's psychological model of Psychoanalysis. The triune of selves in this framework refers to the Ego, the Id, and the Superego instead of the Middle, Lower and Higher Selves.

There are, however, major differences between the two models of consciousness. In psychoanalysis, the Id refers to instincts, survival and sexual energies, limitations to surmount. or get past. Yet, in Huna, the Lower Self includes a wider range of energies, sexual

AND emotional, to be respected, integrated and worked with.

In psychoanalysis, the Superego refers to the "Higher" moral structure, the conscience, socio-cultural values referring to principles of right and wrong, good and bad. However, in Huna, the Higher Self is more concerned with unconditional love and support. The individual learns his or her *own* lessons or values instead of adopting them from outside sources. This is neither Hedonistic nor Narcissistic. It does not lead to anarchy and total selfishness because the one universal law referred to in Huna lore is to commit no harm, no violence.

The rest of the laws and rules we make up as we go through life.

Finally, both the psychoanalytic Ego and the Kahuna Middle Self refer to the identity with self, the "I", with its intellectual and mental capacities. They both deal with the outer world, a "reality" orientation. In psychoanalysis we would wish to develop a strong Ego to balance the Id and the Superego. In Huna we wish to identify more with the Higher Self, and go to that source for guidance, balancing the Middle and Lower Selves.

Analytical Psychology

A later approach, Analytical Psychology, developed by Carl Jung, concerns itself with the Personal and Collective Conscious, the Personal Unconscious, and the Collective Unconscious. The Middle Self with its intellectual basis contains both the Personal Conscious, our Ego and identity, and the Collective Conscious, our interactions with others and our tangible environment. The Lower Self with its memories and repressed or forgotten material relates to the Personal Unconscious, the personal perceptions of everything around us. The Higher Self relates to the Collective Unconscious, cross-cultural and cross-societal perceptions of everything within and around us.

The Collective does not deal with personal memories, but with

Archetypes, "blueprints" of many universal concepts--Mother, Father, Self, Soul, Spirit and/or God, and so on. However, how we approach and identify with the Collective always filters through the Personal Unconscious. In terms of Huna, the Lower Self imposes its patterns and memories upon any perceptions of, and communications with, Spirit. Because of this I have included below both the Personal AND the Collective Unconscious within the Lower Self.

Kahuna Theory

Lono	Ku	Kane
Middle Self	Lower Self	Higher Self
Logical Self	Feeling Self	Spirit
Intellectual Self	Emotional Self	Creative Self
Goals	Memories	Shouldless Parent

Transactional Analysis

Parent	Child	Adult

Psychoanalysis

Ego	Id	Superego

Analytical Psychology

Personal Conscious, Collective Conscious	Personal Unconscious, Collective Unconscious	Collective Unconscious, God Archetype *

We could choose to identify with the fire and brimstone, judgmental, unforgiving God. Yet, the God Archetype we choose to identify with in the context of Huna is the loving, forgiving, limitless and creative force--the Higher Self. As always, the choice is ours *to make.*

In the Jungian approach we develop a strong sense of Ego or individual identity in order to explore and communicate with the deeper aspects of ourselves, not to balance the Id and Superego as in

Psychoanalysis. With enough certainty about ourselves and our identity, we can then let go of the Ego in order to explore our deeper aspects-the Personal and Collective Unconscious, the Lower and Higher Selves.

The unconscious is rich with mythology, both Personal and Collective, and it is within this framework of stories, pictures and symbols, that the Lower Self communicates. We will develop our personal mythologies as they relate to the Lower Self, and explore collective mythology as it relates to the Higher Self. We will look at our creations in the world around us and how they symbolize our thought processes. We will take a closer look at the three selves and how they communicate with, teach, and learn from each other.

- - -

- 3 -

The Soul's Journey

...and once we pass our fear, we move into that realm known as love and beauty, and nothing in this world or the next or next is beyond our grasp.

In the last chapter we touched upon Jung's viewpoint of the personal and collective unconscious. The term "Unconscious" refers to that area of personality that may not, as of yet, be at the level of conscious awareness. We often bring the content existing there to conscious awareness through feelings and symbols, sometimes through the avenue of dreams, visions, meditations, inner dialogue.

It is the Lower Self, the link between the Middle and Higher Selves, that expresses itself in the form of pictures, symbols, stories, "Myths". These myths refer to what reality SEEMS TO BE. And the Lower Self is the one to bring these myths to conscious awareness. It demands attention.

Perhaps this is why one personal goal, according to Jung, is to accept our "Shadow", the negative aspects of our emotions and personal nature. We need to accept and work with our repressed personal material, our fears and memories (good and bad), basic instincts...the Lower Self. In doing so, the personal unconscious will not so easily limit the experience with our Archetypal nature, the Collective Unconscious. Memories of the past will not limit our interactions with the Higher, Creative Self.

The need for both love and courage.

We need to love ourselves and others, to create a safe environment, in order to effectively communicate with the Lower Self, and to allow the Lower Self to communicate with us. Yet, when we open those lines of communication, we will discover thoughts and feelings previously hidden from conscious awareness. Consequently, courage is needed because some of the thoughts and feelings held within the "Shadow" may not seem readily acceptable to the Middle Self. They may seem illogical, out of the framework of our ordinary reality, seemingly foreign. But they are necessary to explore in order to acknowledge the totality of self.

Rediscovering The Relationship With Spirit

One way to explore ourselves safely is through myth and story. In today's complicated and busy environment, we find a renewed interest in this. The collective mythology is cross-cultural in many regards. Creation myths, Rebirth, Spirit, Shadow–all have one thing in common. They all have something to teach us as we journey to self awareness.

In classical mythology, one story, Psyche and Eros[8] (Psyche and Cupid in other texts), stands out amongst the rest. For a complete study of the classical myths I would like to refer you to any of Edith Hamilton's books. However, following is the Steven Rogat abridged version of Psyche and Eros, so please forgive me for any liberties I may take. As you read along, keep the Kahuna model of the three selves in mind. The mortal realm relates to the Middle Self, while the Underworld represents the Lower Self, and Mount Olympus is the Higher Self. As Psyche journeys along, she starts within the perceptions and focus of the Middle Self, shifts to the Lower Self, and finally identifies with the Higher Self. With this shift in attention and identity, Psyche changes as well. She represents the mind in the beginning of the story and the soul at the end. Be aware that Eros changes as well. He represents the heart, beauty and love throughout the story, yet expresses himself differently as the story progresses.

Psyche And Eros

The plot begins with a look at Psyche, a mortal woman living on the Earth. She has grown to womanhood and has become the most beautiful woman many people have ever seen. However, Psyche, being far from content with her beauty, begins to hate it. Many men are afraid to touch her because they feel her beauty is beyond their reach. Psyche herself feels ignored and unworthy. She does not accept her own beauty.

Meanwhile, in another neck of the woods, Aphrodite, the Goddess of Beauty, has become extremely enraged at the attention Psyche has been getting. Calling on her son Eros, the God of Love, Aphrodite instructs him to seek out Psyche and destroy her. He goes along on his merry way, supposedly to fulfill his mother's command, until he sees Psyche. He becomes so captured by her beauty that he falls in love with her and has absolutely no intention of destroying her.

He goes to Apollo, the Oracle or Seer, for help, and the two of them plot to save Psyche. When Psyche comes to consult with Apollo, he tells her that life holds nothing better for her than to marry a winged monster. She should go to a barren hilltop alone to meet her destiny (In another story she resigns herself to death, and goes to wait upon her funeral pyre).

In helpless despair, she resigns herself to her fate and carries out Apollo's instructions. It is at this point that Eros finally goes to carry out his mother's directives. But when he sees Psyche's beauty, he cannot let her be destroyed. and he transports her nearly lifeless body to his mountain palace where they are to live together.

Upon awakening, Psyche finds herself in a darkened room with her unknown savior explaining the parameters of their relationship. He will not tell her who he is, and she is never to look upon him. They are to spend their nights together in the dark. Eros will leave during the daytime, returning only in the evening.

Additionally, Psyche is not to align herself in any way with the mortal realm which ignored her. If she breaks any of these covenants, their life together will be over! Psyche falls passionately in love with Eros (after all, he is the God of Love) even though she doesn't know who he is, and she intends to keep her agreement.

But happy endings aren't that easy to come by here (they rarely are when dealing with Classical Greek Mythology). She starts to distrust the whole situation. With permission from Eros she is able to see her mortal sisters to let them know she is okay and not dead as they had assumed. She tells them of her happiness and prosperity but then does something foolish. She listens to her jealous sisters' advice and decides she must see this being, her lover, for who he really is. After all, suppose he IS the winged monster that Apollo had spoken of?

In the middle of the night, Psyche lights an oil lamp, poised and ready with a knife to kill the "beast". But when she sees Eros she recognizes him instantly for who he is, the God of Love. Being so shocked and distraught at her own folly, she accidentally spills some hot oil from the lamp and awakens him. He is burned by the oil, sees what is going on, and feels so betrayed that he immediately leaves her.

Keep in mind, at this point, that Psyche has thus far just whimpered along, feeling sorry for herself every time there is a decision to make. She ignores her own worth and passively goes along with what others tell her to do-first Apollo, then Eros, then her sisters. But a change is slowly taking place here. She does not accept her fate and, deciding she cannot go back to the life she lived in the mortal realm, she starts on her journey to find Eros.

After many dead ends, she finally seeks him out at his mother's residence. Aphrodite, discovering that her son did not destroy this "wench", becomes enraged and takes Psyche into custody. The Goddess lays before her several "impossible" tasks to be done before she will allow Psyche to see Eros. With each task, Aphrodite, secure in the knowledge that the mortal woman will never complete the tasks within the allotted time frame, leaves Psyche on her own.

Psyche begins each job feeling sorry for herself and gives up on ever seeing her beloved again. But in each instance she receives help and/or instructions from some of Eros' friends who feel sorry for her. She completes each task in turn as she passively follows instructions given to her (old habits are hard to die). Aphrodite becomes increasingly enraged and lays before Psyche one last task at which she will "surely" fail. She is to go to the Underworld, Hades, to pick up a container of beauty cream and return it to Aphrodite.

One of Psyche's first responses is to kill herself. She climbs a white tower, planning to jump to her death. As fate would have it, the tower (representing the path to Spirit) did not wish to see this happen so it gave her directions to allow her safe passage in and out of Hades.

Psyche embarks on her dangerous journey. Following instructions (once again), she goes underground, and pays the Ferryman to take her across the river Styx on her way to Hades. While crossing the river she sees people floating in the waters. However, as ordered, she does not help these people, for they are individuals who could have helped themselves while alive and chose not to.

The crossing accomplished, she gives some meat to the guardian at the gates of Hades, Cerberus, the three headed dog. And while he is distracted, she gains admittance. Still "admirably" following instructions to a tee, she gets the beauty cream and resumes her trek back to the mortal realm.

But lo and behold! While on her journey to the mortal realm, Psyche actually has a thought of her own! She decides that she deserves to have some of the beauty for herself. She will disobey Aphrodite's express instructions not to open the container. And so Psyche, accepting her own beauty and potential, opens the container, only to fall into a "deathlike" sleep.

Eros, who up to now has been in a self-pitying stupor, feels Psyche's plight. He leaves Aphrodite's house and swoops down to rescue Psyche (for real this time). He brings her up to Olympus, where he appeals to Zeus for assistance. Zeus, being well disposed toward Eros, pities Psyche in her distress and admires her endurance. He consents to awaken her and to marry the two lovers, thereby allowing Psyche to join the world of the Gods, herself becoming immortal.

> We can rejoice in the marriage of Psyche and Eros, the marriage between thought and feeling, the mind and the heart.

We draw our own map of growth and enlightenment through learning certain lessons and becoming more aware. We accept our own beauty as the mind and soul become one with the heart. Psyche starts her life within the confines of the mortal realm, continues journeying through the Underworld, and is finally delivered to the immortal realm. The journey must include the three different levels of reality; the decisions and focus of the Middle Self, the feelings, hopes and fears, visions and dreams of the Lower Self, and the benevolence and healing of the Higher Self.

It is only after Psyche has journeyed to the Lowerworld that Eros accepts her *unconditionally*. It is only after he is willing to love and accept Psyche's journey from the Middleworld to the Lowerworld that he combines all his worlds into the totality of self; fulfillment on all levels.

When a Shaman, priest, medicine man/woman, or traveler goes on a journey for healing, enlightenment, or any number of reasons, often that journey leads to the Lowerworld. The journey involves the Lower Self where communications may be in the form of visions, dreams and symbols. However, with the intent to heal, he also draws on the Spirit world, the Higher Self to receive Guidance. "The Shaman thus becomes a bridge between the Lower and Middle Worlds and the Sky Realm."[9] At other times, the traveler may go to the Upperworld or Higher Self on such a journey, but he will also acknowledge the importance of symbols, visions and feelings on this quest.

Again we see the interaction of the various selves. In journeying, we go to the Lower Self with the aid of the Higher Self, or we go to the Higher Self with the aid of the Lower Self. In either case, we leave the ordinary reality of the Middle Self and enter the realm of non-ordinary reality, that of the Lower and Higher Self. This one aspect of the traveler may be the most important distinction between a therapist and a Shaman. The modern day therapist does not necessarily alter his or her own reality in order to do the work and journey with or for the client. The Shaman, however, almost always does

- - -

When exploring the Lower Self, the Lowerworld, "new" territory, we not only need Guidance, but courage as well. We need to let go of our knowledge and understanding of the way things "should" be, and give ourselves over to experience. When acknowledging and exploring different levels of reality, the ego will likely be threatened. The Middle Self, our identity, the "I" that understands many things in our ordinary, everyday reality, must experience a death of sorts. Psyche, on her journey, must get past the three-headed dog which guards the gates of Hell. Might this guardian represent our fear?

Author Carlos Castaneda, in his books concerning mythology and alternate realities, at one point refers to a giant, terrifyingly huge gnat, larger even than he is. However, just as Psyche needed to pass the three-headed dog in order to gain admittance to the deeper realms, Carlos needed to deal with his gnat, his symbolic personal guardian at the gates of HIS Hell. He gets past it in order to explore the different realities available to him, just as we must get past the fear of exploring our own Lower Selves or "Shadow".

Delving deeper in the "Psyche and Eros" story, once past the guardian, while in Hell, Psyche must eat sparingly lest she gets trapped there. This lesson may be a caution to explore our emotional content in moderation. The intention, when exploring the Lower Self, needs to be that of integrating those experiences into the framework of the other selves, not with the intention of getting stuck in the Lower Self.

A similar experience occurs to Castaneda. His mentor tells him that he may have too many fears regarding his own lack of self importance, and to not indulge himself too much in that fear. Carlos is exhorted not to dwell too long on that fear, for he may lose admittance to the deeper realms. And, once admitted, it would be dangerous for him to lose too much of his objectivity, lest he get trapped in that alternate reality.

We've mentioned Hell, or Hades, the Underworld, but what is it that we are alluding to? We've also talked about the dangers of getting stuck there, but what is that danger?

Remember, we are exploring the Lower Self, the child self, with its own set of needs and wants, its own feelings and emotions, dreams and visions, fears, lusts, hurts, angers and memories. Getting stuck in the fearful or limiting side of that world, without the balance of the other realms, may truly be experienced as "Hell". A nice place to visit, but I wouldn't want to live there. We create our own hell if we ignore the other selves, if we act solely out of the Lower Self. More simply put, an uncontrolled Lower Self may be equated with hell and with evil because of its characteristics WHEN TAKEN OUT OF THE CONTEXT OF THE OTHER SELVES.

In context, we can experience our full range of emotions and even our fears with the Guidance and balance of the Middle and Higher Selves. We can meet our Shadow head on, and deal with it. Ignoring it doesn't make it go away; we merely become ignorant.

We can acknowledge and explore the Lower Self, not by itself, but in the context of the totality of our selves.

- - -

- 4 -

The Psychic Accesses: Breathe and Relax Into Spirit

"Now this won't hurt a bit..."
--Dentist's Favorite Saying from
"Preparation For Drilling Handbook"

If we wish to explore new realms of awareness, we need to first let go of our present focus. If we look at things solely from the Middle Self's viewpoint, we are merely perpetuating the Middle Self's control and limited awareness–we get stuck in our everyday, ordinary awareness. To explore and experience our other selves, we need to put the Middle Self aside and let go of ordinary reality. And with that shift in attention, we step outside of ourselves and into the world of non-ordinary reality, viewing the world from a different perspective.

By integrating the focus of the Middle Self with the experiences of the Lower Self and the overview of the Higher Self, we open up to limitless possibilities.

But let's take this one step at a time, so we don't get lost along the way. The first step is to shift our attention.

There are four basic means of increasing the experience of our psyche's journey through the various realms of awareness. These "psychic accesses" are termed Thanatos (death, pain and suffering), Narcos (drugs), Hypnos (sleep or deep relaxation), and Pythos (the wavelike, rhythmic motion of the snake).[10]

Many psychotherapists have the tendency to call all altered or trance states "hypnotic" states of awareness. However, hypnosis is only ONE method of altering consciousness and accessing non-ordinary reality. Because different people respond differently to various stimuli, if one type of access does not work, another one might.

The accesses, however, are not mutually exclusive, and two or more may be used simultaneously. Yet they all have one thing in common–releasing the current focus of the Middle Self. Letting go of our attention upon the tangible, physical, material expression of our thoughts, we leave the physical body behind. We go into the metaphysical realms (that which is above or beyond the body).

Thanatos

When we die, we leave the body. But Thanatos also relates to pain and suffering. When in pain (physically and/or emotionally) we often have the urge to explore ourselves more deeply. We explore the reasons behind the dis-ease, and we often become more emotional. We begin to integrate the different parts of ourselves. The conscious mind steps aside, allowing the subconscious a greater expression.

In extreme pain, we may even instinctively call on Spirit, the Higher Self. Give me the staunchest atheist, a non-believer in Spirit, and even he or she, when in enough pain, may say "Oh, God!". Thanatos is an effective access to our deeper realms and, although it works for many people (myself included), I would not call it the first method of choice.

Narcos

Narcos may also help us to go beyond the body. Whether the narcotic in question is alcohol, marijuana, hallucinogens, or another drug, we may use it in order to access the deeper realms. However, Narcos FORCES the opening to other realms, sometimes at a rate beyond our own control or readiness. Additionally, the connection with Spirit often wears off after the drug loses its effect. We may then find ourselves needing to depend on that drug more and more, until we've become addicted.

Make no mistake, getting in touch with Spirit IS addicting, but we can do it without being destructive to ourselves and our bodies. We can access Spirit in healthy ways. Perhaps this is the reason that some of the most effective dependency recovery therapies are Spiritually based.

When a person is trying to let go of "Narcos", meditation can provide a healthy, alternative access to the metaphysical realms. Getting past the investment in our bodies, our physical environment, does not need to be equated with trashing that environment.

Hypnos

Hypnos, the root word of Hypnotism, literally means "sleep", and being in a Hypnotic trance means to be in a "sleeplike state". Many types of meditation, which I call passive meditations, fall into this category. By allowing the body to relax, we shift our attention away from ordinary reality. Our new focus can now include the deeper realms–the subconscious and Superconscious.

By entering into an altered state, we can then effect, control and help to heal the body. Again, the attention no longer comes from the Middle Self, but from non-ordinary reality, accessing information and energy from all three selves. The object is to bring this expanded awareness back to the Middle Self so that during ordinary reality we can draw upon it. By doing so, we expand the Middle Self's concepts and effect physical reality in more expanded and limitless ways.

Pythos

Pythos is the wavelike, rhythmic motion of the snake. Many meditations, those I call active meditations, fall into this category.

Martial arts, movement exercises, drumming, sexual activity, psychodrama, singing, dancing, breathing and running are but a few. All these exercises have one thing in common: they involve our senses, our body.

Of all the accesses, Pythos is my favorite because we can shift our reality base from ordinary to non-ordinary reality while directly and immediately involving the body. We can "bring Spirit home", involving our whole range of experience–physically and metaphysically. Making the experience more tangible, we journey mentally, emotionally, Spiritually AND physically. Additionally, Pythos can be used to induce Hypnos. Once our attention has shifted to the altered state, we can use that shift to further relax the body, leaving the Middle Self's focus behind.

The Breath: Use It With Intent

Many of the communication and dialogue exercises, as well as the imagery work presented in this text, will be introduced by Pythos in the form of the breath. The reasoning behind using the breath for much of our inner work is simple–it is easy to use. We carry it around with us at all times. We don't need a self-hypnosis tape, a drum, music or any external means of accessing the deeper realms. Although these other tools are useful, fun and more tangible, they are not necessary. We can simply breathe. Having learned to use the breath, we can then use it in conjunction with the other tools to deepen the experience.

While exploring previously unknown territory, we may have a tendency to tense up because of fear, habit or any number of reasons. By tensing the body, we not only affirm that there is something to be afraid of, we also block communication between the Middle, Lower and Higher Selves. In order to explore the Lower Self with its feelings, and the Higher Self with its Guidance, we need to relax. Opening the doorway to constructive communication, we let our thoughts and feelings "flow" through us, allowing ourselves to experience the altered state and expanded awareness.

For simplicity purposes, the Middle Self may be considered to be "located" within the head. That's easy to imagine, since the Middle Self relates to the conscious mind—our thoughts, logic and intellect. The Lower Self, however, relates to the deeper feelings and memories, the "repressed" part of our being, the subconscious. Because this is considered to be "below" the Middle Self, we can look at this as being deep within the core of ourselves. When we talk about having a "gut feeling" about something, we are referring to the Lower Self's reaction to a given situation. When we have just been "hit in the gut", we have tensed up after spontaneously accessing the Lower Self's feelings, beliefs and memories.

The next step is to relax, to get the energy back to the center, to Breathe! Over the years many of us have gotten into the habit of not breathing deeply. This may be due to emotional reasons such as stress, fear or limiting thoughts. Or it may be the result of a physiological condition such as pregnancy, illness, or accident.

Unfortunately, with a decrease in the breath we may inadvertently institute one of two downward spirals. The first spiral, already mentioned, involves our emotions. An emotional response causes us to decrease the breath. Having less breath, we tense up, resulting in a decreased ability to access our emotions. Being out of touch with our emotions, we may limit the possible responses to any given situation. With these limitations we may then create other limiting situations, resulting in tension and a decreased breath response, more tension, less breath, more tension, and so on.

This spiral is now in full swing and will continue until it collapses. Usually this collapse will be in the form of emotional and/or physical pain. Thanatos will take over. We'll leave our bodies, touch our Spiritual nature, and then return to the body and to physical reality. The end result is that we will access non-ordinary reality. We become refreshed, and then come back to ordinary reality. Hopefully we will not merely "jump into the fray" again.

The second spiral relates more to the physical body when there is an illness, accident or dis-ease. Our physical reaction to a situation causes us to take in less breath. Creating additional tension, we have decreased our energy reserves within the body. This lack of energy may then prevent healing from taking place as effectively as possible.

Then again, with the prolonged dis-ease, we may instinctively once again decrease the breath, continuing the dis-ease, and hindering the healing process. I do not know which comes first, the chicken or the egg, the dis-ease or the shallow breath. But we can at least learn to stop the downward spiral.

Instead of unconsciously hindering the breath, emotional response-ability and the healing process, we can cultivate the habit of breathing deeply, both consciously and intentionally,. We can use the breath for several reasons: as a cue to the Lower Self that it will get loving attention, as a means of healing, and as a means of focusing attention upon the deeper realms. Breathing deeply, we relax. Relaxing, we affirm the safety to explore new territory. Feeling safe, we set the stage for increased emotional and physical responsiveness.

Webster's Dictionary defines Yoga (a Sanskrit word) as a practice involving compete concentration upon something, especially a deity, in order to establish identity of consciousness with it.[11] There is one type of breathing exercise, Yogic Breathing, that I have found to be invaluable when relearning how to breathe.

With the breath we can better communicate with the Lower Self and seek Guidance from the Higher Self. We can also focus the Middle Self's thoughts and the Lower Self's feelings upon a state of health, vitality, and freedom. Bringing in more life force, manna, into our bodies, we free up our thoughts and feelings, release our limitations and identify more closely with Spirit, the perfection of all that is.

The Yogic Complete Breath[12]

Yogic Breathing entails getting the breath to ALL parts of our torso. It entails breathing deeply, first to the abdomen, then to the diaphragm or Solar Plexus, to the chest and finally to the upper chest. Optimally, this would be done with a wavelike, rhythmic motion–Pythos.

Lie down or stand comfortably, allowing the torso (upper body) to be straight yet relaxed. Breathe in through the nostrils and out either through the nostrils or the mouth. First, practice breathing into the abdomen, having the abdomen expand with the inbreath and fall with the outbeath. You may even wish to place one of your hands upon your abdomen in order to feel its rise and fall.

After raising the abdomen, raise the diaphragm. Place one hand on the abdomen, the other on the diaphragm to insure the breath is reaching the intended parts of the body. Practice this for several minutes if you need to in order to get it "right". This may take several practice sessions in order to feel comfortable. When assured you can raise your abdomen and diaphragm with each inbreath, you can continue the wave by allowing the chest to rise and fall with each breath.

Finally, to complete each inbreath, raise and pull back your shoulders allowing the breath to reach your upper chest and lungs. This completed breath is not jerky, but rather relaxed and natural, simulating a wavelike motion starting at the abdomen, continuing through the diaphragm, and then through the chest and upper chest. (Note: you may feel the abdomen contracting slightly upon completing the inbreath, and that is normal.)

After holding the breath for a mere second or two, exhale slowly, relaxing each of the relative body parts, all at once, or in succession: first the upper chest, then the chest, diaphragm and abdomen. Breathe deeply, filling up the entire torso, hold for a moment, then relax further with each outbreath.

The Breath Adds Life!

The reasons for cultivating this type of breathing are many. First, we can practice it until we can take a complete Yogic breath comfortably and easily at will.

We can take ten of these breaths, while lying down on the way to sleep, allowing ourselves to rest more quickly and completely. Ten breaths, while standing, when awakening from sleep, will help us to "rise and shine" more quickly and easily. Note that if we do this breath while sitting, the abdomen becomes folded up and does not allow freedom of movement. We can compensate for this by having the hips higher than the knees, while sitting on a cushion, chair or bench. This allows the back to straighten and the abdomen to have more freedom in which to gather the breath.

As the breath becomes more comfortable, it may be used for any number of things, in any number of situations. We can use the breath merely as a means of relaxation. Yet, I recommend it more strongly as an introduction to, or during, meditation, centering, internal dialogue, exercise, etc. Additionally, we can use it during any emotionally stressful situation. As the breathing apparatus loosens and tones up, we have the benefit of being more aware of the breath, not only when it is deep, but when it is tense, shallow or restricted. When physically or emotionally stressed, we can use the breath to relax and restore our energies. This helps to prevent dwelling on fears and/or limiting thoughts. We can relax and increase our response-ability within ANY situation.

Basic Relaxation Exercise

To train yourself to relax faster, more easily and more completely in conjunction with the Yogic Breath, find a private space and try the following exercise.

Sit or lie down comfortably.

Take a few deep breaths, relaxing on each outbreath.

Take a deep breath, hold it while tensing up EVERY part of your body. Let go of the breath and relax...

Breathe in. Hold it while tightly squeezing both eyelids shut. Release the breath and relax.

Envision a light switch atop each eyelid. Take in another breath, and on the outbreath flip those switches off, shutting off the tension, creating a state of relaxation. On the next inbreath create a switch in the middle of the forehead. Shut the switch off on the outbreath.

With each successive breath create a switch while inhaling, and shut it off while exhaling. Continue with the face, working down the entire body–each side of the jaw...the mouth and lips...the neck...both shoulders, elbows, wrists, hands and fingers...the chest and upper back, abdomen and lower back...hips, knees, ankles, feet and toes.

When complete, scan your body (starting with the eyes) to see if there are any stubborn spots, places that have tensed up again, places where the switch has turned itself on again. If you find a stuck spot, breathe, create the switch and shut it off. Will yourself to relax on the inbreath. Let yourself relax on the outbreath.

When totally relaxed, stay in that state for a few moments. Enjoy it.

To come back to the here and now, keep your eyes closed and make some sort of physical movement: stretch your arms, move your feet or head, rub your face, anything to reconnect with your body. Then, after a moment or so, slowly open your eyes and return completely.

- - -

Practice this exercise frequently, for several days or even weeks, until you can relax at will. You may find that doing this exercise before any other meditation is helpful. The major benefit of this exercise is to get the body's concerns out of the way, allowing for deeper exploration. Another benefit is to simply increase awareness of the body's responses to different situations. When it becomes tense, relax it. When you realize your breathing is shallow, you can be fairly certain that you've just tapped into physical and/or emotional stress. Breath deeply and relax, if not at the moment, then whenever you remember.

When filled with energy and totally relaxed, we are ready to participate more fully in whatever we do–meditating, exploring relationships, communicating with others or ourselves, focusing our attention, feeling, living, loving.

- - -

- 5 -

Grounding

...yet, were it not for its strong roots,
the tree would not be able to lift up
its mighty arms toward the heavens...

Whenever we try something new and different, we extend ourselves by putting forth the effort to see, understand, grow, learn and feel. In expanding our awareness, we try to better understand our environment to see what *our* part is in creating that environment.

In identifying with the Middle Self and its awareness, we identify with the physical environment–both external (referring to our surroundings) and internal (referring to our bodies). We identify with what is consensually known as ordinary reality. Yet, as we grow toward a new and expanded relationship with our surroundings and our bodies, we reach BEYOND the physical body, beyond the Middle Self's focus of attention, beyond the "I" that we identify with. We enter non-ordinary reality, the world of the "meta-physical", above or beyond the physical.

Increasing our focus to include what is "beyond" or "out of the body" relative to the focus we have had within the body, we increase our "out of body" awareness. But we still need to function within the parameters of the physical environment, addressing the practical, everyday concerns of ordinary reality and expressing ourselves within the physical realm. We need to get back down to Earth--to "Ground".

In doing so, we may at times try to get back into the old habits, the old perceptions, the old "I" with which we've become comfortable. However, more often than not, we incorporate new perceptions and experiences that lead us to a new center. We redefine relationships with our physical reality. In short-we change.

Our center of attention, the "I" that we identify with, constantly undergoes change.

Affirming that we can ground and get a new center, we know that the connection with the Earth, and with the Middle Self's focus of attention, is still available. Knowing we can ground at will allows us to safely explore new territory. This knowledge permits fluidity of movement between ordinary and non-ordinary realities. We can explore, then ground, explore, then ground.

In another context, when we try to get closer to another person, to better understand or to help, we increase the amount of energy we put forth outside of ourselves. We may lose ground, we may lose our center. Whenever we get emotionally involved with someone or something, we start identifying with that person or thing that is "outside" of ourselves. We let go of center.

So how do we find it again, even if it IS a new one? How can we be "ourselves" and still expand outward? How can we safely let go of ground and then find it again? The answer to these questions is simple: We just do it by getting back to center. We ground.

Some people prefer to call this process centering, some prefer to call it anchoring. You may wish to call it one of these names, especially if you were "grounded" a lot as a child when you did something wrong. In this case the word "grounding" may have some limiting memories associated with it. However, the term I prefer to use IS grounding because it is descriptive of the relationship we have with our Earthly existence, our physical reality.

Folklore and mythology have numerous references to this idea of grounding. The witch's broomstick, for instance, represents the grounding cord, the connection with the Earth. She leaves the Earth with the aid of the broomstick and holds onto it for safety, AND for her return to the Earth.

Theseus And The Minotaur

In classical mythology, the story of Theseus and the Minotaur also refers to the grounding process. Theseus, a mortal man, decides to go into the maze where sacrificial youths and maidens are to be slain by the Minotaur, a being which is half-man and half-bull. However, before going in to save the maidens, a mortal woman by the name of Ariadne gives him a ball of golden thread. He is to unravel this thread behind him as he goes deeper and deeper into the labyrinth. Upon completing his mission, he can follow the thread back out of the maze to safety.

The youthful maidens represent our innocence, feelings, sensitivity and awareness, the feminine energies relating to the emotional realm. The Minotaur represents death, not only of the emotions but of our connection with other parts of ourselves as well. And yet, tempting death, we must go into the maze to search for and rescue our feelings.

As instructed, we can take our experiences back with us, rather than getting lost in the maze and lost to death. We can follow the thread, the "grounding cord", back to relative safety, back to ordinary reality.

The Usefulness of Grounding And Acting From One's Own Center

Before describing the specific process of grounding, I would like to convey more of the meaning behind it, its uses, and reasons to master it. Grounding is certainly useful when dealing with our emotions and with the journey to self awareness. But it is also useful whenever we deal with the balance between physical and "out of body" energies.

Shock

You are walking along the street and a car has a tire blowout right next to you; you react instinctively, emotionally. Fear takes over, you get startled, you "jump out of your skin", you leap into alternate reality. What do you need to do? Ground! You can actually shorten the adrenalin rush and aftereffects of shock dramatically by merely focusing your attention back within the body. Instead of shaking nervously for the next fifteen minutes, you can ground. Releasing that out of body energy instantly or within a couple of minutes, you bring yourself back to your body.

Shifting Awareness

You are hiking in the mountains or standing upon a tall building. You look down, and the world seems to spin. You start to lose your balance, you fear you'll lose your footing. What has happened here is simple. When you looked down or into the distance, you sent a good part of your conscious awareness into the distance. The energy outside of the body suddenly increased relative to the energy within the body. You experienced what may be called the "out of body spin", the sensation you feel when you leave your body "too fast".

In classical mythology, the spiral staircase addresses this out of body spin. If you'll remember, one of the last things Psyche did before entering Hades was to climb the spiral staircase in the white tower. Go up that staircase too fast and you, too, will become dizzy. So you left your body too fast, you became ungrounded. What do you do? Ground! Instead of actually losing your footing, you can increase the amount of energy connection with the Earth and regain your balance. I am all for a communion with Spirit, but not necessarily while standing on the edge of a precipice.

Emotional Grounding

Emotional stress may also cause us to be ungrounded. Sometimes we have a vague sense of something being out of place... It's a normal day and you're going about your business, but things seem just a bit out of synch. You start a project, but because of your lack of focus it becomes incomplete even before you start. Or perhaps you are physically active and every table, chair or door is just waiting to reach out, grab your foot and trip you up. "Extraneous" thoughts keep getting in the way. You wish you could get enough awareness back to what you are doing, long enough to complete something safely. You wish you wouldn't stub that same toe three times before the end of the day. Ground!

Feeling Other People's Feelings

You are in an emotionally charged situation and things seem to escalate beyond your control. You are with someone who is angry and you get angry. You are with someone who is sad and you find yourself feeling sad. His or her pain becomes your pain. You may wish to understand someone else's feelings better, but now you understand them too well...you feel them. You may have a hard time discerning whose pain is whose, which feelings belong to the other person and which ones belong to you. You may leave that situation and, hours later, find yourself carrying that other person's feelings and energy around with you. Ground!

To illustrate how easy it is for us to literally pick up another person's feelings, please refer to the following diagram.

We are in an emotionally charged situation and our emotional level is a certain amount (A). The other person we are with has a higher level of emotional involvement (B). We feel the other person's energy, and we raise our level of involvement (C) to match his (hers). He feels our increase and raises his level of emotion (D) to match our increase. Then we raise our level (E) to match his. He matches our increase. We match his level and so forth and so on.

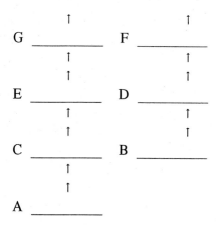

This situation can escalate beyond control, even within a relatively short period of time. This is wonderful in the case of loving, happy or sexual energy. With a "contact high" we may not wish to ground. But what if that energy consists of sadness, pain, or anger? It may be in our best interest to ground and to approach that situation from OUR center rather than from the other person's. We may better handle the situation if we increase the amount of energy WITHIN the body relative to the energy OUTSIDE the body.

Grounding Versus Shielding

Some people, when faced with negative energy from others, prefer to "shield". When they start picking up on someone else's pain, anger or sadness, they may surround themselves with an impenetrable bubble or perhaps imagine a mirror reflecting back the other person's energy. There are some teachers who encourage this as a means of psychic self defense. But I cannot support this in most situations.

Getting into the habit of shielding can be detrimental. We may become numb and cease to be aware of others' feelings.

With shielding, we may cease to be sensitive to our surroundings, separating ourselves from our own environment. By grounding, however, we can still be open to others and our surroundings, yet affirm the ability to let go of negative energies whenever necessary. In Serge King's book, *Urban Shaman*, he makes a distinction between the "Warrior Shaman" and the "Adventurer Shaman", and this distinction may very well apply to ANY conflict. He states that "a warrior shaman tends to focus on the development of power, control, and combat skills in order to deal with fear, illness, or disharmony." By contrast, an adventurer shaman deals with these things "by developing skills of love, cooperation and harmony".[13] The warrior shields. The adventurer grounds.

To protect ourselves from conflict and negativity, we can shield ourselves or we can ground. Shielding, we may try to change the other person or reflect back the negativity. However, this may create a never ending battle in which we are caught trying to outdo each other. It likely will not end the conflict and may even escalate it. Grounding though, we can let others have their own feelings. We do not try to change them.

With grounding, we let ourselves experience the full range of emotions, affirming that we are safe and loving regardless of the conflict. We stay open to the energies around us without getting caught in a pattern of continually protecting ourselves more and more as time goes on. Affirming our own center, we can simultaneously affirm someone else's. The other person feels less threatened (hopefully). Cooperation is gained more quickly and easily.

Shielding may be equated with stubbornness and the ability to "not be budged". This can lead to the inability to compromise. Grounding, on the other hand, may be equated with certainty. And being certain, we know we will not compromise too much, and therefore remain free to resolve conflict more easily.

The first time you decide to try this meditation you may wish to have a friend read the directions and guide you through it. You could also tape record it and then play back the tape to yourself. It is not a complicated meditation, but it is best done with as few external interruptions as possible. While you prepare for this exercise, review the reasons for, and benefits of, doing it. Then review them again, mentally, while you do the meditation.

The Grounding Meditation

Sit comfortably on a chair or stool with both feet flat on the floor and take a few slow, deep, centering (Yogic) breaths. Just relax. You can use the relaxation exercise from the previous chapter. Breathe all the way down to the tailbone, the root center, the connection with the Earth. Continue to breathe fully, slowly and easily.

Now, see the point at the bottom of your spine, and lower a rope or cord from that point, down through the chair, into the ground. Lower and lower it goes, through the soft layers of the Earth, through the hard layers, the watery layers, all the way down until it's just hanging above the core of the Earth, until it's dangling above the molten core of the Earth.

Secure the cord at the top where it connects with your tailbone. You can nail it, safety pin it, tie it, glue it. You can even have five Dwarfs up there holding it. However you wish to secure the cord is fine. Make it fun. It will be easier to do, and you'll want to do it more.

When it's secured at the top, lower it the rest of the way into the Earth and secure it down there. You can tie it, glue it, make it an electrical cord and plug it in. You can make it a chain and anchor it, a tree with its roots deeply embedded within the Earth, anything!

Take three slow, deep breaths. With each outbreath let the cord get a little wider until it's exactly as wide as your body. WILL it to get wider with each inbreath, and LET it get wider with each outbreath. If it does not want to get as wide as your body right now, that's fine. It will when it needs to, and if it wants to get wider than your body, that's okay too.

The cord is now widened a bit and safely secured at both ends. Feel the Earth give that cord a tug, just a little tug to let you know it's there.

Take another slow, long, deep breath. Make this one very slow and deep. On the outbreath take any tension, any excess energy, any energy that isn't yours and flush it down the cord. Just let gravity take it away to be cleansed by the Earth. You can repeat the last breath if you feel the need. Feel the lightness, the relief. Feel your weight being settled into your tailbone.

Before you open your eyes, it is best to make some kind of physical movement. Move your feet against the floor, stretch your arms, move your head around, rub your face with your hands. Do any kind of physical movement to bring you back to the here and now, back to your body. And, when you're ready, gently, slowly open your eyes.

The first few times you do this exercise you might find yourself a little lightheaded. This is a temporary effect. It will probably not happen after doing the meditation several times and is nothing to be concerned with. Remember, first we shift our attention to an altered state, and then we reconnect with ordinary reality.

- - -

Ground To Get Grounded

When we are asleep, the majority of our consciousness is out of our bodies, and this exercise will help to get our feet more firmly on the ground (figuratively) before we need to do it (literally). I recommend grounding every morning (or whenever you arise from sleep) for a week or two, until you can have the experience clearly in your mind and body. The object is to "program" the subconscious mind with all the feelings and associations related to grounding.

When the meditation becomes an integral part of yourself, you can perform the whole meditation in one breath. On the inbreath, lower the cord, secure it at both ends, and widen it. On the outbeath, feel the tug and drain away any excesses. Furthermore, when the meditation only takes one breath, you can do it while you are walking, talking, driving, or at any other time you may feel the need.

Ground To Focus On Emotions

Grounding is especially useful when involved in an undesirable, emotionally charged and escalating situation. By grounding, we can stop the escalation, or at least take response-ability for our part in it. We can take a deep breath and ground, stopping ourselves from getting carried away by our own and others' emotional responses. Whatever energy or emotional involvement we shed was probably not ours in the first place. Whatever is left over is definitely ours, and we can take response-ability for it.

Grounding AFTER the situation can also be helpful. By putting the brunt force of that emotional encounter behind us, we can enter new situations, positive or negative, without the burden of the past.

Grounding In Therapeutic Situations

As therapists and healers, we extend our energy and our consciousness to include those we are helping, we increase our out-of-body energy. We extend our energy, consciously or unconsciously, to include the other person and, therefore, become somewhat ungrounded. If we find ourselves too emotionally involved during the session to assist therapeutically, we can ground. At the very least, we want to clear ourselves of the client's energy before moving on to anyone or anything else.

As the helpee or client, during an emotionally therapeutic situation, or during meditation, we are delving deeper into ourselves. While doing this, we may have a tendency to get caught up in our own emotions, becoming ungrounded. At other times, in a physically therapeutic situation, we may relax and detach ourselves from our emotions and/or our body, once again becoming ungrounded. By grounding we reintegrate body and feelings.

In any case, if we need to get back to the response-abilities of the everyday world, we'd better be in our bodies and have a little surety as to where our feet are headed. Like Theseus who followed the golden thread in order to find his way out of the maze, we can do the same.

Grounding For Children

The above grounding exercise, in all likelihood, is probably too complicated, not to mention boring, for a child to do. So I would like to share several images or stories that may be appropriate when relating to children.

One such image is that of a tree. A tree, by necessity, has roots, and needs to stay put for verrrrrry long periods of time so he or she knows exactly where to get food, water and sunshine. It would be very nice indeed to be able to move around quickly, hopping from one place to another, but the tree would soon tire and grow weak. Every so often, the tree needs to take a deep breath and look down, deep into the Earth, thanking itself for its strong roots, and thanking the Earth for holding on to those roots. On the outbreath the tree can then look up again, stretching its arms, and feeling the strength and the warmth of the sun.

Another image is that of Herman the worm. Worms come up out of the ground periodically to explore new territory. But it's not good for them to move around too far, and of course, too fast, because they may lose their way, and lose contact with their other worm friends. So, mostly, Herman just needs to know when it's time to go back down under the ground. He can take a deep breath and go back down, feeling the warm Earth all around him giving him a hug and sending him its love. When he lets go of his breath, he can come back up, moving merrily along on his way with more strength and courage.

After telling the story of the tree or the worm we can come up with a hand signal, some nonverbal massage that we give to the child that means "take a deep breath and look at your roots. Remember your tree nature". Or, "take a deep breath, remember the worm, and look around under the Earth, feel the warmth and love and strength. And on the outbreath, come back up, look around, and feel the love and warmth and the strength you've just gotten from the Earth."

Another image, shared by Don Meichenbaum (Cognitive Behavior Therapy) at one of his seminars, is that of a turtle who, on the inbreath, withdraws into his shell and looks around at the nice tidy home he's got. On the outbreath, he comes back out with strength, warmth and the ability to move about more slowly and carefully to play with his other turtle friends.

We can relate the story of the caterpillar who needs to go into its cocoon before it can be as free and as beautiful as the butterfly. Feel free to improvise on any of these stories. Better yet, tell all the stories (with proper embellishments, of course) and then ask the child which one he or she likes the best.

An important point needs to be made here about the hand signal that you devise...the child needs permission to give you, the adult, the same hand signal whenever there is a need for YOU to ground. In this way the child will not only have a means of centering, but also a healthy means of feeling powerful.

Reminding a child to ground can be useful whenever he or she appears overwhelmed by feelings of anxiousness, fear or anger. Following a skinned knee or scary bicycle accident, grounding can also help him or her safely return to the body.

Grounding Others

As a helper, healer or therapist I can draw on my knowledge of grounding in order to be more effective in a wide variety of situations. If I can ground myself, I can ground others as well. However, I had better be sure I am grounded first! The whole process simply takes two breaths instead of one. On the first breath I ground myself. On the second breath, while breathing in, I visualize the other person's cord being lowered, secured at both ends, and widened. While exhaling, I envision the tug and see any excess energy or tension in the other person being flushed down the cord.

After a therapeutic session, whether this be of a psychological or a physical nature, I first ground myself. I can then ground the other person, allowing him the opportunity to return more fully to his body. If the helpee is in a prone position (as is often the case with therapeutic body work, breath work or meditation), I can visualize the cord being lowered from the whole body rather than just from the tailbone area.

As a parent dealing with a child, especially one who may have hyperactive tendencies, I can ground the child. Even when dealing with adults who may be having a hard time slowing down enough to deal effectively with a situation, I can use this technique. Again, first I ground myself, then I ground the other person. This is not close to a permanent grounding, but it may slow the other person down just long enough to do something and/or listen more effectively. It may slow them down enough to help them through a tough mental, emotional or physical challenge. It may even help to stop an emotionally charged situation from escalating beyond control.

By using the grounding exercise, I focus MY intent to stay on track, and I give the OTHER PERSON a chance to be grounded.

Next time you're driving and you see someone who may be a drunk driver, ground yourself and then ground the other driver. I have used this technique many times and almost never cease to be amazed. The other driver will slow down, drive straighter, or even pull off the road, either on the shoulder or at the next exit.

Taking this technique one step farther, if I can ground someone else, I can also ground objects in order to institute a firmer connection with the Earth energy. If I am driving on an exceptionally slippery road, I can ground myself and then the car, either from the center of the car or from each of the tires. Importantly, I first ground myself.

It may not be proven that this technique has any effect on another person or object whatsoever. But, at the very least, it allows me to be more relaxed and able to deal more effectively with any given situation.

Ungrounding

In that we can ground objects, we can also unground them. I would first ground myself, and then simply unground the object. I can see that object with its own grounding cord, envision a pair of scissors in my hand, and then cut the cord. When lifting a heavy object, this technique lowers my own center of gravity and makes the object seem lighter.

To be totally fair to this subject, I must mention the possibility of ungrounding people as well as objects. When dealing with a physically threatening situation, I can use this to give myself an edge. Once again, I would ground myself first, and then unground the other person by cutting his or her cord, thereby unbalancing my opponent. I mention this because it may be useful as a defense mechanism, but only as a last resort. This cannot be taken too lightly, nor should it be used to control a situation unnecessarily! If the other person were to hurt himself after I have cut the cord, I would feel responsible. I would have that person's injury hanging over my head. This is one of those times in which I need to be especially aware of my intent.

The question has been posed as to whether or not we are breaking others' free will by either grounding or ungrounding them. However, this would be dependent on the circumstances. If I am a helper, therapeutically treating someone, he or she has already given me permission (directly or indirectly) to manipulate the energies. Yet, if I choose to ground a person who has not expressly given me that permission, then I need to be especially aware of my intent.

Do I intend to manipulate another's energy out of malice, out of love, because of fear, in the name of healing, or for protection? These are questions that only the individual can answer, and these are actions that the individual must answer to. As with anything in life, there is no action without its consequences. What is the intent?

Grounding Is A Choice

There are times when we, ourselves, may choose to be ungrounded. To be grounded at all times seems like a rather boring existence. Freeing ourselves to explore the Spiritual or emotional realms, giving or receiving a healing, or making love, are but a few of situations where being ungrounded may heighten the experience.

Once, while at an amusement park (famous for simulating and/or creating the out-of-body spin), the Ferris Wheel did what it always does. It stopped while I was at the top. Becoming dizzy and nauseous,

I grounded myself. Unfortunately, I then became extremely bored and didn't get my money's worth of fear! As another example, I would not ground myself while experiencing a Spiritual, emotional or contact high unless it became dangerous or I became irresponse-able.

Affirm your ability to be grounded at will!

Knowing that we can ground easily allows us to venture further into ourselves and into the world around us. Knowing that we can gain more "control" at any given moment, we can feel safer in letting go of some of our control. Letting others get closer to us, we can share more of ourselves with others, empathizing and understanding more.

We can feel freer to explore our thoughts, our feelings, our needs and wants, our environment, undiscovered mysteries. And within a safe environment, we can find the guidance necessary to get through the maze of self-exploration.

- - -

- 6 -

Asking for Guidance, Listening to Self

I looked up. I looked down. I looked all around. In a frenzy, I looked everywhere, and the sights were truly a-maze-ing. Then I saw the Light.

There are many theories, beliefs and dogmas regarding Spiritual Guidance. Some schools of thought put their energy behind Jesus, some deify Siva and the 1,001 Gods. Others revere Buddha, Mohammed, Allah; God manifest in many forms. There are many who believe that there is no reason to contact Guides, angels or specific forms of Spiritual Guidance, saying that "God is the only one to believe in, and that's all there is to it."

That's great but, personally, I am not even going to pretend to understand what God has in store for me or for others. I am going to look within for a personal connection with Spirit, and with that part of me that IS Spirit, the awe-inspiring world of creation and manifestation.

Whatever image, or concept we assign to the Higher Self, WE are the ones choosing a form with which our Middle and Lower Selves can identify. If we are Spiritual, we are connecting with that Source and that Guidance. If we adhere to a certain religion, then THAT is the set of rules we have adopted in order to communicate with the Higher Self. Recognizing that everyone chooses the set of rules which works for him or her personally, we can maintain a sense of understanding and respect for any and all beliefs systems.

Spirit: In Whatever Form Is For The Highest Good

The Higher Self, the "Great Parent"[14] in Huna, is the authority guiding and connecting us to Spirit and the Spiritual nature. We need not give up our personal belief systems, be they Jewish, Hindu, Christian, Atheist, Buddhist, Agnostic, Moslem, and so on, in order to become aware of and consult with this loving, healing energy. We are still empowered by learning how to work with our Higher Self.

There are some schools of thought that believe we only have one Spiritual Guide. Other systems say we have seven Spirit Guides, no more or less, some say we have many. My personal experience is that we have several, more or less, that are with us for long periods of time, more or less, with several, more or less, that come and go in order to teach us and to help us with specific lessons.

On a psychological level, we may not have any personal Guides at all. They may be archetypes. They may be illusion, a distortion of ordinary reality. They may be personifications created by the Lower Self, appearing in forms we can relate to and communicate with more easily. They may just be a product of our active imaginations, things we make up in order to feel better about our selves and our world.

On a Shamanic level, though, everything has Spirit; guides are Real within the framework of our Spiritual or non-ordinary reality. Everything, each being, whether it be human, animal, plant, earth, water, fire or air is alive. Each entity has a certain spirit of its own, a personal spirit, as well as a "group" Spirit. For example, each deer would have a specific spirit, it would be THE spirit of THE deer. However, there is also the spirit of Deer, the Higher Self or Spirit of all deer. On a Spiritual level, we com-municate with everything around us, everything communicates with us.

Everything is in relationship!

I have met many guides, many spirits, some of which are people, animals, or angels. Some take indistinct forms, and some take very specific forms. We can receive Guidance from these spirits during meditation, sleep, journeying or other means of accessing nonordinary reality. We can also be in touch with them during "normal" everyday reality. Imagine a hawk helping you find your way out of the woods, a deer preventing you from hitting a cow with your car, a butterfly helping you appreciate the beauty of nature, the Light leading you to a place you need to be. These things are wonderful when they happen. Appreciating them, giving them a powerful place in your life makes them happen more.

Relationships with the world of Spirit can be as real as the relationships we have within ordinary reality. At times they can even be more rewarding because those relationships are often on a deeper, more personal level. The "trick" is to be able to integrate the two worlds, making the tangible relationships we have more Spiritual, and the Spiritual relationships more tangible.

Throughout each experience in the world of Spirit, we can remind ourselves to be thankful. Starting and finishing each experience with blessings and thanks, focusing our intent upon healing and whatever is for the Highest Good, we can call on Spirit in whatever form we relate to. I have chosen, and prefer, the White Light, to represent the Higher Self, the connection with Spirit or God. This is so because the Light can be used in more diverse ways when meditating. We can empower the Light with our thoughts, to represent the Highest possibilities available, encompassing unconditional love and acceptance, the Creative Force. We can then stay open to receiving Guidance in whatever form(s) it takes. If we have gotten into as loving a state of mind as possible, if the intent is pure, then whatever form Guidance takes must be the right one for us.

Getting in touch with Guidance is rather simple. Trusting it, though, is a lifetime endeavor.

Getting in touch with Guidance is a matter of using one of the psychic accesses discussed previously, with the INTENTION of focusing on Guidance. With the shift in attention we go beyond our everyday world, beyond the intellectual framework we exist in much of the time, beyond ordinary reality, and into non-ordinary reality.

As with the Psyche and Eros story, there are three levels of non-ordinary reality: the Middle World, the Lower World, and the Upper World. And there are various descriptions of, and uses for, each of these realms. King describes the Middle World as "the Garden", a private place you create with your imagination out of memory or desire, and to which you go...for rest, healing, insight and adventure.[15] The Lower World or Underworld is "a place of challenge, where obstacles or difficulties in the form of monsters, magic, and natural elements stand between you and that which you seek. The quest usually consists of getting past them, reaching your goal (usually a power object of some kind), and bringing the object back."[16] The Upperworld is a "place to get inspiration and divine assistance from...those personified forces of transformation which can take many forms and play many roles."[17]

Various descriptions of these realms generally agree with one another. However, there are some differences among practitioners regarding which realm to go to, and for what purpose. King recommends going to the Upperworld to meet Spirit helpers in animal form. Yet Michael Harner, in *The Way Of The Shaman*,[18] describes journeys to the Lowerworld to access your power animals. I prefer to meet my power animals in the Lowerworld because the Lowerworld seems more connected to the Earth and nature spirits, as are animals. However, you may relate differently to each of the realms. Go with the intent of healing, and then go with whatever works.

In Huna tradition we can go to the Garden (in the Middleworld) and find a hole in the ground for access to the Underworld, or a hole in the sky for the Upperworld.[19] Yet Harner refers to having direct access to the other realms. For instance, the Lowerworld can be found through a hole, a tunnel, a cave, a tree trunk or similar entrance. We can go directly from ordinary reality into ANY of the three realms of non-ordinary reality. One of the "Psychic Accesses" discussed earlier is used to first connect with non-ordinary reality.

Then we have a choice of where or when we go.

Additionally, King states that "the quest to (the Underworld) is not done for understanding. You can get (that) in the Garden. The quest is done to change the fundamental idea structures that are in the way of healing."[21] This is true when clearing the resistance and fears to growth, and when identifying more with Spirit. Yet, I find we can also use the Lowerworld's experience in order to understand our own personal processes of change.

Regardless of the above discrepancies, journeying and receiving Guidance is a personal experience. Going to the Middleworld first may be easier for many people because that is the realm most similar to our own reality. As a place out of memory or imagination, it is most easily accessible. In the majority of hypnosis sessions, a person often goes there first, to the private garden, safe place, or power spot. In Shamanic journeying, we go up or down from there. In therapeutic situations we bring information and experience into the Middleworld. In Shamanic journeying we go beyond the Middleworld for information and experience. In reality (weird term to use in this particular discussion), we can go to whichever place works for us, and use the experiences in the best possible ways for our own lives. With Guidance, the intent of the journey will take us to the proper place at the proper time.

Following are several of my favorite Guidance meditations which are simple and easy to follow. Read through each exercise completely before doing it. If you haven't done any of these exercises before, you can have someone take you through them, or you can put them on audio tape for yourself. After the initial journey, you can improvise on any meditation in order to fit your personal needs. You can go directly to the other realms, or to the Middleworld first, and then to other realms. You can meet your power animals in the Lower and/or Upper Worlds, or simply ask for Guidance in whatever form is perfect for you.

Guidance Meditation: Middleworld Journey

Sit or lie comfortably. If you wish, use a drumming tape to more easily keep you in the altered state, or merely to keep you "on track". Using the Yogic Breath, do the relaxation exercise.

Call in the Higher Self, surrounding yourself with a cocoon of White Light, and focus your intent on healing.

Create an elevator in front of you–old or new, big or small, wood or metal. Just make sure it is sturdy and safe. If you have a problem with elevators in ordinary reality, you may use an escalator or stairs.

As the door closes, you can see out the little window in the door. You're on floor # 10 and, wishing to go to the first floor, you press the button for # 1. With each outbreath, relax, and see each floor rising above you through the window; 9, 8, 7, 6...This elevator may even be found in your body, with the tenth floor being located in your head, the first being in your abdomen. Now continue to take the elevator down; 5, 4, 3, 2, 1...

After the elevator stops, open the door, and you can see your own private little garden spread out in front of you. There's a path at your feet. As you start walking down this path, look around and be aware of your surroundings. This is YOUR private space, totally safe, totally yours. If anything threatens you, manipulate it, change it, or change yourself so it no longer poses any threat whatsoever. You are totally safe.

Walking down this path, focus on the intention of finding your own power spot. Don't look for it. Just keep walking and be willing to sit down in that spot when it appears. If it does not present itself, create it! It can be a place out of memory and/or imagination. It can be a place you've been to before, or some place totally new.

After sitting down, see another path stretching out before you toward the horizon. Call your Guidance and wait. On the horizon you can see forms, indistinguishable at first. But, as they come closer, you can make out sizes, and perhaps shapes. Feel the safety. This is your space. These are YOUR Guides and will never harm you. Let them come closer. You can now see how many of them there are. Are they all people? Is there a power animal, a personal animal ally, that may help you in both non-ordinary and ordinary realities? Are they tall or short, thin or heavyset, male or female?

Thank them for coming, and ask if there is one who would like to speak with you. See that Guide coming forward. If it is hard to see that Guidance clearly, try focusing on his or her feet. When you can identify details in the feet, move up the legs, then the torso, then the head. Be patient. You will eventually see that particular Guidance, if not now, then perhaps during a future session.

Whether or not you can see the Guidance clearly is not that important now. When you FEEL his (her) presence, ask if there is a name that he or she would like to be called and if there is a message for you. If a name is not forthcoming, ask if you can come up with a name. After doing so, ask if that name would be acceptable. Ask if there is something with which the Guide is here to help you. What could you do in your life that would be for the Highest Good of yourself and all concerned? The answers may come in the form of words, feelings or symbols. Is there a lesson that you are here to learn?

Do not ask, "Will this happen?" or "Should I do this?" It is better to ask question such as, "What energies surround this situation? Is it for my Highest Good to do this? Is there anything in particular that would be good for me to explore? Is there something I need to know to help myself and/or others?" Dialogue with Guidance. Do not dwell on trivia. Guidance is available for important issues, not to be abused or ignored.

When it is almost time to go, see a "magic treasure chest" before you. There are three gifts for you within that chest. Reach in and take a gift. What does this gift represent? Is there some way in which this gift applies to your life or to that of someone around you? Reach in and take a second gift, then the third. What do they represent? Does one gift explain the meaning of a previous gift? Do they all represent a personal process? Accept the gifts from Guidance. Affirm the intention of using those gifts only for the Highest Good.

Is there anything else your Spirit Helpers wish to communicate at this time? Is there a sign that Guidance wishes to use in order to let you know of his or her presence in your everyday life? A tap on the shoulder, a cool breeze over one part of your body, a twinge in one of your muscles, the presence of something in your external environment–a feather, a cloud form, a certain bird or animal demanding your attention? These are all possible signs. Affirm that you will be open to recognizing his or her presence in the future, and that you will take a moment from your life at that time to reflect on a particular situation, emotion or set of thoughts.

Again, thank them for coming, and reassure them that you will be in touch later. Say your good-byes, and let them depart the same way they came, seeing them getting smaller as they approach the horizon.

Affirm that you will access this space again, more easily and more successfully each time you do. Remembering to take your gifts, start walking back toward the elevator.

Enter the elevator, close the door and press the button for the tenth floor. On each inbreath you rise one floor; 2, 3, 4, 5...As you take the elevator from your abdomen back up to your head, you gradually return to your body, to the physical reality. You remember everything that occurred during this session. You affirm the intention of applying any knowledge gained to your daily life.

- - -

When first doing this exercise, some of the information may be confusing or indirect. You might not relate to some of it. However, at a future date, something gained during this meditation may prove useful. An animal may represent certain characteristics to be explored, or it may represent a Shaman, Power animal or Guide in animal form. This is natural. We may meet one Guide during one journey, while meeting a different one at another time.

Things may happen that do not necessarily fit what we think is the "norm", but we can gently explore these areas at any time. My own process may shed some light here. Upon doing the Guidance Exercise the first time, there was a Guide that would not show himself. I knew he was there, hiding behind a tree, but I could not identify him.

Over the course of a YEAR, this Guide would sometimes show me an arm or leg, or even whisper incoherently. I knew on a deep level that this represented a part of myself I refused to look at. However, one night, while dreaming, he appeared. Within the dream, I was being chased by a group of aggressive people and felt I had to get away. I ran faster and faster, seeing no escape, when suddenly I heard a "pssst". I stopped and saw a man standing in the shadow of a tree. When I asked who he was he introduced himself as "the Guide that had been hiding (from me) all this time". He said that I hadn't been ready to listen to him up to this point, but that I was now ready to both listen to him and to deal with a certain situation in my life instead of running from it. He was here to help me with that.

To be sure, sometimes guidance comes in mysterious ways. Once I discovered the specific name of this particular Guide, however, I did not stop there; I explored the lesson he had to teach and then when it was time, moved on, leaving him behind.

Discovering the specific name of one of our Guides does not mean we should call on that Guidance at all times.

For instance, we would not wish to call on our English teacher for advice in Math. The same applies to personal lessons. We do not need counseling in business if our lesson relates to more personal issues. And, we cannot be certain that our lesson pertains just to one area or another. Calling in the Light and focusing our intent on whatever is for the Highest Good allows the appropriate Guidance to communicate.

Even if we do like to focus on a specific Guide, we can still see if there is any other Guidance that wishes to speak. For example, we can ask our Spirit Animal to help us contact another Spirit Helper, one that may be appropriate at that particular point in time. We can then be open to any additional information needed. Do what works for you. Do not limit the results. Improvise when necessary.

Lowerworld Journey

Another journey involves the Lowerworld, that place of challenges or obstacles to be overcome, possibly a place of memories needing to be healed. You can do this journey after accessing the Middleworld and your power spot, or you can go directly from ordinary reality into the Lowerworld itself. After breathing and relaxing, find a place out of memory or imagination that leads into the Earth - a cave, a tunnel, an elevator, a tree trunk, anything you relate to. My personal Lowerworld access is a freshwater spring issuing forth from the Earth. In ordinary reality it's only two inches high, but in non-ordinary reality I shrink to fit. Anything will work. Just be sure you return to the Middle Self and everyday reality by the same means you journeyed down, or you may become disoriented and ungrounded.

Focus on what you wish to accomplish on this journey. Put it into words to focus your intent more clearly. Some Shamanic practitioners feel it is necessary to state your intent aloud four times in order to clearly focus. This is a good rule of thumb because it really does help clarify the purpose of the journey.

Remember, this is still YOUR entrance to the Lowerworld. Nothing belongs there except what belongs there. Any threat can be dealt with instantly, lovingly, and effectively. Affirm you protection, your strength and courage as you delve into previously unexplored areas.

Now enter the Lowerworld. Ask for Guidance, perhaps asking directly to meet with your power animals or animal allies. Go on a journey. Some practitioners feel that if a certain animal shows up four times on this journey, then you may accept it as a power animal.*

Some practitioners do not go on ANY journey without a power animal protecting and guiding them. This may be a good idea, the purpose being that of creating safety and the feeling of being protected. Upon gaining access and meeting your Guidance, ask questions as in the previous journey, or dialogue in whatever form seems appropriate. You may even ask if there is something you need to experience, and go on a side trip. Is there another guide you need to meet? If the answer to either of these questions is yes, then let your initial Guide take you to where you need to go.

Experience, dialogue, learn. When it is time to end the journey (when the drumming ends if you are using a drumming tape and haven't returned yet), give your Guidance thankfulness, perhaps a gift, and ask if there is something you can do to help heal someone else.

When it is time to come back, again, return by the same means you entered. Remain still and silent for a few moments. Then slowly move your body and open your eyes.

In some traditions, it is considered to be important NOT to accept a reptile or insect as a power animal or spirit Guide because they may represent illness and dis-ease. But, in other traditions it is okay. Personally, I have a hornet as a guide and, although it does represent fear and distress, I have made friends with it. I work with it. It's rare that I work with my hornet in relation to others, but on occasion it feels right to do so. I recommend using caution. The only reason I use my hornet is that it "chose" me. I merged with it in the dreamstate, and it became a guide of mine before I even knew what I was doing. I accepted my limitations, and I worked with them. Just use caution when a reptile or insect shows up.

Dream Visions

Be aware that our Guidance may show up in the dream state as well as in meditation. They may come in the form of people, animals, plants or other elements. Sometimes it is fairly obvious that a certain person or animal is truly Guidance. At other times it may not be so obvious. If during the dream state we have merged with, become, or been totally surrounded by a particular animal, we may be fairly certain that that animal IS a power animal or animal ally.

Even the most nondescript animal has power. It is not size that matters, it is strength. For example, during one particular ceremony, a Native American sweatlodge, one of the participants called on her power animal and in the vision a mouse showed up. She did not like having the mouse as a power animal because of her judgment that it was not strong enough, so she ignored it. But think about it. A mouse can hide easily. It can eat almost anything. It can blend in with its surroundings. It can make its home almost anywhere. I'd be proud to have a mouse as an animal ally. Imagine her surprise when, lowering her head to the ground and lifting up the edge of the canvas covering the lodge up to get some fresh air, she met a mouse sleeping not three inches from her nose! That mouse slept there for hours. When we finally dismantled the sweatlodge to let it dry out, the mouse finally awoke. He looked up, asked if it was time to go, and walked away.

In some dreams you may find yourself being chased or threatened by an animal. Do not take this lightly. It may signify a power animal's strengths and abilities trying to catch up with you. Psychologically speaking, being chased or beaten by people during the dream state may signify a part of you or a part of your past that may be trying to catch up with you. Even falling and/or dying is significant. I tell students to work with these images. First see how they apply to your life. Then reprogram the dream!

On your way to sleep, whether that is five minutes later or the next night, hold the previous dream's image in mind. Say to yourself, "I let them catch up, (or I can fall, or die) and I am totally safe." Repeat this to yourself as you imagine it to be so. Know that you are totally safe. Whether it is your past trying to catch up with you, a part of yourself dying, or your future trying to prepare you for what is to come, let it be so. Be more whole. That's the worst that will happen.

Upperworld Journey: Guidance And Healing Meditation

Another method of getting in touch with Guidance involves going to the Upperworld rather than to the Lowerworld. I have combined this journey with a healing meditation, but you can use it at any time with or without the healing. Improvise at will.

Sit comfortably. Using the Yogic Breath, do the relaxation exercise. Use a drumming tape if desired.

Focus on the White Light, the Higher Self and Unconditional Love.
If you wish, go to your private garden and power spot.

Using your Grounding Cord, ground and affirm your connection to the Earth. Feel your awareness, with each breath, rising higher and higher. Identify more with the Higher Self. Expand yourself and your energy, first looking down upon your body, then upon your meditation space, your environment and surroundings. As you go up through the clouds, look down upon the Earth.

Feel the infinite space and limitlessness around you. With complete peace of mind, you encompass everything. You are a part of everything. Everything is part of you. Your body is made of Love and Light. Look down upon your Light Body, see and feel its perfectness. While in this Higher State, ask for a message or anything that may help you to heal your body and your environment. Is there a particular Guide that wishes to speak with you? Is there anything to be shown to you that would be of importance? Dialogue. Journey. Explore...

Thank yourself for experiencing this state, and thank your Higher Self. Now bring any information you've received with you as you slowly start your journey back to Earth. See and feel your grounding cord extending down to the Earth below. Slowly start returning to the Earth within your Light Body, your perfect state of health.

Your Light Body is getting smaller and smaller as it approaches the size of your physical body, and you stop, just above your physical body. Spend several minutes and massage any tense spots with your Light Hands. Send those parts energy, healing them, turning them to Light. Feel your Light Body merge with your physical body, looking inward to see that everything within has turned to Light.

Breathe slowly and deeply. Feel the grounding cord tugging at your tailbone, your connection with physical reality. Deeply embed the Light Body into the physical body. Relax, and breathe in the health you feel right now.

Stay in that state of awareness for several minutes. Feel Spirit within you, and ask how you can apply the energy and information you've just gained to your daily life. When you are ready to emerge into ordinary reality (come back through your private garden if you went there first), gently move a part of your body, rub your face, move your legs a little, stretch your arms, make some fists and relax. Feel the Light and the strength coursing through your body. When you are ready, open your eyes. See the world around you as perfect, and be willing to carry the feelings of Love, Light and Healing with you throughout your day.

- - -

There are many ways to improvise this meditation. You can take the elevator up ten floors instead of down, climb a ladder up, take an escalator, ride on the back of a bird. You can go to the Middleworld first or directly to the Upperworld.

There may also be a silver cord emerging from the back of your neck in the physical body. This cord connects the physical body to the etheric or Spirit body. You may use this cord in addition to the grounding cord. You can ask for one or more gifts, or just information. You may wish to continue a conversation from the last meditation. Do what works.

No matter where we go, or what we do there, it is the intention and the focus that are of utmost importance.

As you practice this exercise, as well as exercises like this, you may not need to spend as much time centering and relaxing; things become easier with repetition. Writing down or recording the experience gained from this meditation is also useful. Some things may not seem important at the time but may be important later. Anything that happens or appears to happen during meditation is significant. The Lower Self often communicates through symbols. Although we may not recognize the meaning of a particular symbol instantly, it may become clear later.

Is This My Perception Or My Imagination?

I've encountered the following questions many times. "How do I know whether this message, this thought, is from my Lower Self or from my Higher Self? Is this my imagination, what I want to think, or is it real?" Though the answer to these questions may seem rather disappointing, here it is anyway...We don't know! We can seem to know. We can think we know. We can feel the rightness of any message. But we cannot, with one hundred percent certainty, know.

Perhaps our Lower Self is getting in the way when we think we are talking with our Higher Self, perhaps not. Sometimes the Lower Self, because of its fear of not getting enough attention, or of not getting what it wants, will try to pass itself off as the Higher Self. Sometimes we may hear what we want to hear, not what we need to hear. However, focusing on a purely loving energy, the Higher Self, we "raise our vibration level" to the extent that we are truly more in touch with the Higher Self. When we feel in touch with our Spirit Guidance, there is a good chance we are.

More specifically, the Higher Self will often answer a question before we are even finished asking it. We can then double check the answer by asking the question in a different way. On a purely semantic level, the Lower Self may hate the question, "Should I do this?" Shoulds almost always bring up resistance and rebellion. And the Lower Self, because of the emotional charge and memories just accessed, may get unnecessarily involved. It will offer ITS answer in lieu of the Higher Self's answer. However, if we phrase the question, "Is this for my Highest Good?" or "Would it be to my benefit to do this?", the Lower Self does not respond in a negative manner. The Higher Self's answer then comes through more clearly.

The Ideomotor Response:
Training Your Body to Tell Your Truth

We do not always need to be in a deep meditative state in order to access Spirit. When in ordinary reality, we can simply breathe deeply, center and relax. We then ask the Higher Self to give us a sign when contact is made, and that sign can be in any number of forms. Some examples may be: experiencing a spontaneous twitch in a muscle, a shudder going through the spine or through another part of the body, a tingling sensation, a cool breeze over a part of the body, or a flash of color before the eyes. This contact is still transferred through the Lower Self, the unconscious, and its control of the body. However, if we affirm that we can get great benefit from the Lower Self's support, it will give that support.

Once contact is made with the Higher Self, we can ask the body for an "Ideomotor Response", a form of language in which the body can express thoughts and ideas. We can ask for a "yes" and see if there is a physical response. If so, then we can ask for a "no" and be aware of any response. Having an unconscious twitch in one finger may indicate a "yes", while a twitch in another finger may indicate a "no". The eyes, when closed, being raised spontaneously upward may indicate a "yes", while a "no" would be indicated by a movement downward. In a recent training through the American Society for Clinical Hypnosis it was even recommended that we have a third answer, prompting a third ideomotor response. This category is simply, "not ready to answer yet". For years I did not use this third option because it never occurred to me. Then for a while I didn't use this option because I felt it was a way of avoiding an answer. However, at times I do use it because some questions just don't have simple or readily available answers.

If there is no natural response forthcoming, we can "program" the body to give us the answer in a yes or no form. We can start by centering, calling in the Higher Self and surrounding ourselves with the White Light. We then ask the Lower Self to cooperate with us in this endeavor, convincing the Lower Self that this exercise will be for his or her benefit. Focusing on which part of the body we'd like the answer to be reflected in, such as the fingers or eyes, we say aloud, "this is a yes", and move a certain muscle. We can repeat this process over and over again until we feel we have successfully programmed the body to give us a "yes". Continuing, we repeat the process with a different movement, stating, "this is a no". We can then go to the "not ready to answer yet" category and program that response.

After double checking several times, we will have a reliable, tangible means of receiving Guidance in this form. Of course, the Lower Self, with its emotional investment, may still have a tendency to get in the way and give us false answers. But surprisingly enough, if we just ask the Lower Self whether or not it is lying to us, it usually tells us. Additionally, if we get an answer that just doesn't "feel right", we can ask something to the extent of, "Is it because of my fears that you gave me this answer?" And we will probably get the truthful answer to that question as well.

The Pendulum And the Ideomotor Response

The process of using ideomotor responses can be applied to the use of a pendulum as well as the body itself. The make-up of a pendulum is usually that of a small rock, a piece of wood, a ring or other jewelry, a crystal or other object, hanging from a string or chain The premise for the effectiveness of the pendulum is the same as for the body itself. The chain or string is held in the hand and becomes an extension of the body. The subconscious tends to make minor, often unnoticeable movements of the muscles in the arm and/or hand thereby moving the pendulum in response to certain questions.

We can hang the pendulum in front of us, keeping the arm and hand relaxed, and ask for responses similar to those used with the fingers or eyes. "Yes" would swing the pendulum in one direction, "no" in another direction. "Not ready to answer yet" or "I don't know" would elicit yet a third response.

As stated earlier, I like to avoid questions such as "will such and such happen?" There is one major reason for this: the future is not written in stone. It can change because of our free will and choice, or because of others' free will. It can change because what is for my Highest Good presently may not be for my Highest Good at a future date. It can also change because, having received Guidance, knowing my life is headed in a certain direction, I may have the tendency to just sit on my butt and wait for the future to unfold, effectively stopping the flow of energy.

I still need to feel my way through the present and act accordingly, responding to life as it responds to me. It is easier to move something that is already in motion than it is to move something that is stagnant and unmoving. If I do not put forth the energy, I may get none back. If I put the energy out there, it will most likely be directed appropriately.

Feeling Good Versus Feeling Right

Some things that feel good don't necessarily feel right. And some things that feel right do not always feel good. If I were to make a choice, I would go for what feels right. The logic for this is rather simple. If something feels good, but doesn't feel right, and we still go ahead with it, it may NEVER feel right. But if something feels right, even though it doesn't feel good, eventually it WILL feel good because it was right. Optimally, things will feel good and right simultaneously, and we'll never have to read this paragraph over again!

This line of reasoning is most important when seeking the guidance of ANY teacher, whether he or she is a traditional counselor, psychic, or trance medium channeling messages from "beyond". One of my teachers, Doctor Duran (channeled by Trina Kamp), once said, "Just because someone is dead, doesn't mean they know any more." There are plenty of "dead" people out there who may just like to hear themselves talk. Even if a medium is channeling the Higher Self with its Love and knowledge, the Lower Self may still get in the way, as might the Middle Self with its Ego. In either case, it is not always possible to say with complete certainty that the information gleaned is always correct. "Question Authority."

Many of the judgments about seeing a psychic or "new age" consultant, or ANY helper, might rest on the tendency of the person seeking help to abrogate response-ability to the consultant. The Kahuna teach that every human being is response-able for his or her own actions and the results of those actions. With this in mind, we then have the freedom to seek Guidance and advice from many different sources and in many diverse forms. But, WE must decide for ourselves which information is useful and applicable, and which is not useful. The bottom line is, "Does this feel right when applied to my life-my relationships, feelings, needs, goals, decisions or actions?"

Acting with Guidance and "right feeling", we can explore and experience our lives more fully. Seeing more clearly what and how we create things within our lives, we gain meaning, clarity and direction.

- 7 -

Prayer, Affirmation & Manifestation

Whatsoever ye shall pray for,
believing, ye shall receive.

- The New Testaments

Getting in touch with our Lower and Higher Selves is just the beginning of the journey. The next step is to manifest change within the environment–better relationships, a better job, more comfortable living space, more peace. Relying on Guidance, we can interpret our environment as a reflection of our thoughts. We can know which things need to be accepted just as they are and which things need to be changed, both internally and externally. We can also receive Guidance in focusing on the proper goals to pursue.

There's a saying, "Watch out what you ask for because you just might get it." This is very important to acknowledge before putting a lot of power behind our goals. It is important to decide which goals would be for the Highest Good and which goals would, on the surface, be tempting but, in reality, be limiting or hindering.

Once we generate the proper goals, we then enter the process of manifestation. The Middle Self focuses on a goal, putting forth a prayer or request, whether it be material, emotional or Spiritual. We may want a meaningful relationship, more money, guidance, a good feeling about our lives, and so on. But that prayer must first pass through the belief system, memories and habits of the Lower Self before it reaches the Higher or Creative Self for manifestation. Yet, what happens if the Middle Self asks for one thing, and the Lower Self believes in and affirms something different?

Without agreement between the Middle and Lower Selves, we may just get a jumbled mess when trying to manifest something.

"You always get what you ask for."

We've all heard THAT ONE before, and at times, may have been disgusted when we've heard it. I know I have. The process looks a little like this, "I feel I've gotten something rotten, the short end of the stick. Of course I never asked for that rotten thing so how could anyone in their right mind dare tell me that I got what I asked for? I mean, how ridiculous!" Yet no matter how much we may detest this process, it shows itself over and over again in our lives.

The Higher or Creative Self does fulfill our requests, our wants, needs and wishes, but IN ITS COMPLETE FORM-with the input, not only from the Middle Self, but from the Lower Self as well. The prayer from the Middle Self must be balanced, even outweighed, by the belief of the Lower Self, in order to effect the desired change within our lives. We must believe in AND affirm the reality and existence of what we pray for. For how can we receive what we pray for if we do not believe we will or should get it?

Is it okay to receive it? Can I receive it? How will I receive it? What was my past experience with this? Do I deserve it? The answers to these questions need to be explored when wishing to release any limitations that may attached themselves to our prayer.

There are several methods of exploring the Lower Self's belief system with its thoughts and feelings. I would like to present two ways of doing so. The first is to just simply look at our environment. One of my teachers drummed the following statement into my head, "The end result is our best teacher."[23] This is true when considering that the Lower Self's beliefs will manifest tangibly within the environment. Learning how to interpret the thoughts behind our physical reality leads us to discovering the Lower Self's beliefs.

The second method of exploring our thoughts and feelings involves dialoguing or talking with the Lower Self. Doing so, we can challenge any limiting thoughts or memories, changing them and attracting something better in our lives.

To understand this process of interpretation and manifestation, I'd like to refer to a psychotherapeutic model developed by Albert Ellis called Rational Emotive Therapy or RET (also referred to as REBT or Rational Emotive Behavior Therapy). In his "A - B - C" theory of personality, the Activating Event (A), something within the environment, is perceived, interpreted and processed according to one's personal Beliefs (B). This results in a feeling, an emotional Consequence (C), and then effects the ways in which we act upon the initial activating event. Our actions then have an effect on what we create for ourselves within the environment. The creation is considered to be another Activating Event (A), starting the whole process over again; Activating Event (A), Belief (B), Emotional Consequence (C), A, B, C.

A person's task or goal within this model is to Dispute (D) the personal beliefs in order to create more positive feelings and therefore more positive and effective actions.

Don Meichenbaum, a proponent of Cognitive Behavior Modification, focuses his attention more on our beliefs and stresses the idea that our cognitions are "Cognitive Events".[24] Not only would an environmental situation be considered an activating event, but a cognition, a belief, a perception or goal would also be an activating event in and of itself. In this model, not only something external, but something internal as well, acts as a catalyst, starting the process of "event, belief, feeling, and action". What we think about, and how we respond to our own thoughts and feelings, are significant factors in creating the world around us.

Please refer to the following diagram for these cognitive-behavioral approaches.

Cognitive Behavioral Approaches

```
   (A)              (B)           (C)                  (A)
Activating -------- Belief ------ Emotional ---------- Action,
  Event,              ↑           Consequence       Environmental
Cognitive             ↑                             Consequence,
  Event,              ↑                             Activating Event
Thoughts,             ↑
  Goals               ↑
                (D) Disputing
                 Intervention
```

- - -

We can expand on this further within the context of Kahuna Theory. Please refer to the following diagram which includes RET, Cognitive Behavior Modification and Kahuna Theory.

The Kahuna Model

```
Middle Self ----------------- Lower Self ---------------- Higher Self
     (A)                        (B), (C)                  Manifestation,
Activating Event --------- Belief & Feeling, ---------- Our Actions,
  Cognition,              Cognition & Emotional           Activating
    Goal                      Consequence                    Event
  |------------------------------|
               ↑
               ↑
```

Middle Self's Response to the Lower Self's Reaction, to our own actions and to the Higher Self's Manifestation. Options:
1) Affirm and/or Ignore → The same or similar outcome
2) Dispute and Challenge → A changed (better?) outcome

- - -

The Middle Self is ALWAYS involved in this process!

The Middle Self has a thought, goal or prayer, and the Lower Self adds its beliefs and feelings. It is then up to the Middle Self to respond to those beliefs and feelings. If the Lower Self's response is "okay", we can either affirm and/or ignore it, in which case we will probably manifest what it is we want.

If the Lower Self's beliefs, feelings and memories are not in accord with our wishes, we had better dispute and challenge those beliefs. For if we ignore those beliefs, we will probably manifest either what the Lower Self wants or a combination of the Middle AND Lower Self's wants. Challenging those beliefs, we can hopefully assure a more positive outcome.

The Lower Self's response to the Middle Self's thoughts is, in and of itself, an activating event. The Higher Self's manifestation is an activating event as well. Understanding how the Higher Self manifests the Lower Self's beliefs within the physical environment gives us the perfect opportunity to identify any undesirable outcomes. We can then go back and challenge whatever thoughts and feelings may be standing in the way of creating a better reality.

The Higher Self is also ALWAYS involved in this process! WE Create Our Reality!

In the psychotherapeutic models presented, our actions attract and create our environment. However, with the addition of Spirit, the Higher Self becomes the Creative Source. The Higher Self receives the message from the Middle and Lower Selves and then manifests our thoughts and feelings in the environment Thus, what we experience as a result of our actions is really a result of our thoughts, feelings, beliefs AND actions.

In psychotherapeutic terms this process may be called "magical thinking" and is based on superstition. Although it does not indicate a diagnosis of "mental illness", it is frowned upon in many circles. As I mentioned previously, the negativity surrounding magical thinking may be more societal rather than psychological. Magical thinking just does not fit into some aspects of western culture.

The belief that our thoughts alone can effect our environment and other people brings up a "red flag" on various psychological assessment tools. However, with a firm belief in Spirit, the Creative Force, many people are challenging the validity of these assessments.

- - -

The Middle Self's goals and prayers lead to the Lower Self's response and affirmation, resulting in both action AND the Higher Self's manifestations. These in turn demand a response from the Middle Self, then the Lower Self, and once again, the Higher Self.

This concept may become clearer by looking at a situation from my own life. Although the story deals with manifesting something on a material level, in this case a car, the same process applies when attracting other things such as a job or relationship.

The Car Story

Many years ago I was living in Boulder, Colorado, relying on my bicycle and the public transportation system in order to get around. I enjoyed it, but it was also time consuming and tiring. I started to pray - to ask the universe for a car. My Middle Self put forth the prayer. I then wanted my Lower Self to experience the good feelings about this. I affirmed that I was attracting the perfect means of transportation: I praised my present means of transportation (my bicycle and public transport) and acknowledged my previous cars and the positive feelings they generated from my past. I then wished to manifest those feelings more tangibly in the present and future.

Focusing on those past feelings, I brought them to the present and expanded them until I could feel them being accepted by the Lower Self. Focusing on the ultimate delivery of that car, and "seeing" it coming within a few weeks, I affirmed that I would present myself with a car for my birthday, a wonderful gift to myself.

In this way I put forth the Middle Self's goal to the universe. At the same time, I talked with my Lower Self. I attempted to reinforce and affirm the Lower Self's belief that I had already manifested some of what I want, and that I could create even more.

I had no idea what I had unleashed on the universe but, as things started to happen, I knew it packed a wallop. Within a week one of my friends asked me to help out at his record store while he was to be gone on vacation. I agreed but, since the store was out of town, I would certainly need transportation. He offered me HIS car in order to make the hour's drive everyday. THAT was the beginning of what I call the "cosmic joke" I was honored to be a part of.

Several days later another of my friends approached me. Would I like to drive him to the airport, use his car, and then pick him up after his two-week visit with out-of-state family? Of course! Life was taking an interesting turn here. Knowing I was watching creative thought in action, I watched closely to see what would come next.

A week later another friend asked me for a "favor". She needed a lift to the airport and since I had a car (or two), could I please take her to the airport and pick her up when she returned? Upon agreeing to do so, she also asked if I could watch her dirt bike for her while she was gone. And OF COURSE I could ride it if I wanted.

I awakened on the morning of my birthday and looked upon my creation–two cars and a motorcycle parked in a previously empty driveway. Now for the cosmic joke...a week later, after returning all the vehicles, my driveway was once again empty.

– – –

I felt I was forced to take a good look at my environment and at least partially see how it symbolized my thought processes. I realized that the complete thought received by my Higher Self stated, "I am attracting the perfect means of transportation (Middle Self's goal), but please don't let it be my own (Lower Self's response)." For whatever reason, my Lower Self did not want a car of its own.

Birthday # 1

Middle Self: "I am attracting the perfect means of transportation."
Lower Self: "But please don't let it be my own."
Higher Self: "Okay, Steve (Middle and Lower Selves), here are two cars and a motorcycle, but return them in two weeks."

Realizing what I had manifested, my next step was to dispute the Lower Self's response to my request. I then suggested a different response to my Lower Self, complete with belief and feeling.

Middle Self: "I am attracting the perfect means of transportation. It can be my own."

But it was not to be! I did get a response from my environment, but it was not the response I wanted. Over the course of the next year, I spent much energy looking at this situation. I still acknowledged that I already had the perfect means of transportation, my bicycle and public buses, but I also wanted the form to be more specific to my wants. I wanted a car, one that I could keep. I wanted the perfect car and affirmed that it would present itself at the perfect time.

I asked my Higher Self to help me on this. I affirmed that I would get the perfect car at the perfect time, but not before I was ready, not before my Lower Self agreed with the request. I also affirmed that this goal was on my life's path, whatever that was at the time.

I looked at many cars, but they didn't feel right. I would see a car I liked, but additional expenses would arise, preventing any such purchase. I would miss the "perfect" car by an hour or so. I almost bought a car, but it turned out to be a lemon. I felt the universe was against me! I even reworked the affirmation.

Middle Self: I am attracting the perfect means of transportation. It can be my own AND reliable."

That was no good either. Getting a car was proving to be difficult.

Meanwhile life went on. Throughout this process, I was also wishing to relocate out of town and continually ran into resistance there as well. Finding the perfect place to live was also becoming an insurmountable chore. I finally gave up trying to push my way through the challenges. Disappointed, I felt I had no choice but to commit myself to being in Boulder, to not moving. I committed myself 100% to my work, family and friends.

I dialogued with myself, this time regarding a new place to live. I discovered a Lower Self fear that if I moved I would be lonely. I explored more deeply, talked often with my self (Selves), and finally came upon something, a previously hidden belief: "If I have my own reliable means of transportation, I'll leave friends and family. I'll be lonely." This limiting thought reflected some fears I'd had about moving. My Lower Self did not want to be lonely--therefore, no car.

Middle Self: "I am attracting the perfect means of transportation. It can be my own and reliable."
Lower Self: "But please don't let it be my own and reliable because I'll move. I'll have to leave friends and family. I'll be lonely."
Higher Self: "Sure, here are many distractions, many things to prevent you from getting your own, reliable car, and from moving."

My Middle Self was praying for a car, but my Lower Self didn't believe it to be in my best interest and was afraid to manifest one.

I then affirmed the belief that "I can be with friends and family wherever I am". BOOM! A few days before my birthday (remember my previous birthday?) someone gave me a car!

Birthday # 2

Middle Self: "I am manifesting the perfect means of transportation. I can be with friends and family wherever I am."
Lower Self: "Okay."
Higher Self: "Okay."

The process above may have seemed long and complicated, but the end result was certainly worth it! Sure, at any time I could have forced my will upon the Lower Self and gotten a car. But the process of forcing my will takes a lot of energy and willpower and does not necessarily clear any of my limiting thoughts.

Forcing the issue could have been the fastest remedy in the short run. But ignoring my Lower Self would only have gotten harder over time.

Getting a car before I was ready may have resulted in one or more limiting manifestations. Getting an unreliable car, paying on a car loan I couldn't afford, moving before I was ready, or moving and then being lost and lonely are but a few of the ways this could have turned out. Paying attention to my Lower Self may have been harder in the short run, but as resistance cleared, things only became easier and easier.

When the Middle, Lower and Higher Selves are in agreement, our will has a power of its own. Things become effortless. Magic becomes natural.

Whatsoever I shall pray for, believing, I shall receive.

- - -

- 8 -

The Reality of Symbols

...and I am propelled into a world of colors, a world of shapes and meanings that stagger the mind. To find my way, I need to open my eyes, to explore the beauty that surrounds me. All becomes clear.

The Lower Self relates not only to words, but to pictures and symbols as well. Words are useful to the Middle Self when focusing thoughts and communicating with the Lower Self. However, we can also use pictures effectively when dealing directly with the Lower Self. These symbols keep the Lower Self's interest, and allow the Lower Self an additional means of communicating more effectively with us.

When ASKING a child how he or she feels, we may not get a direct answer. If we ask in words, we might just get a shrug of the shoulders or a blank stare. However, if we look closely enough at the symbols being used we can perceive the child's feelings. What is the tone of voice? What is the body language telling us? What symbols is the child using? What is the story being told? He or she IS communicating, not verbally, but symbolically.

If we ask a child to draw a picture of something or someone, we can get an accurate picture of that child's thoughts and feelings. From the shapes, sizes, textures and colors, from the symbols used, we open up an avenue of expression and communication with the child. The same applies to the Lower Self.

All we need do is communicate with, and listen to, the Lower Self on a level that is acceptable to the Lower Self. If we tell a child a story and then ask that child which of the characters in that story he relates to or feels like, we get a very clear, detailed answer. The child, or Lower Self, will use the story and its characters as symbols with which to communicate.

Life is a story. The Lower Self will use the environment to express itself and to reflect its thoughts and feelings. All we need to do is listen (see) and interpret the environment as a reflection of our thoughts. Remember, the end result is constantly teaching us by giving us tangible information about our thoughts. Therefore the pertinent questions to ask regarding our environment are: What did we manifest? When and how did we create and/or attract it? What are the consequences and results of those manifestations?

Looking at the car story again, the car symbolized mobility, and having my own car symbolized freedom. The mobility and freedom taken together represented moving and possible loneliness. Once I released the fear of loneliness ("I can be with friends and family wherever I am.") I was then able to manifest the symbols of mobility and freedom (my own reliable car).

Whether looking at our thoughts through dialogue or through symbols, keep in mind that our perceptions are always filtered through the Lower Self.

Even Guidance received from the Higher Self is filtered through the Lower Self. The Lower Self uses whatever means are available to communicate with us! So, let's learn to work within the Lower Self's reality system, lest we find ourselves lost in the maze.

Working within the Lower Self's reality system is exciting and has several benefits: (1) We can explore ourselves and our environment more deeply by discovering what symbols the Lower Self uses. (2) By making more symbols available for the Lower Self's use (by expanding our symbolic systems), we teach and allow the Lower Self to communicate with us in a wider variety of forms. (3) We give ourselves a more personal relationship with our environment.

Many times a student or client will say to me, "It's easy for you to interpret my visions, my environment, meditations and dreams because you've been doing this for a long time. But what about me? It's hard for me to do it." It is at this point that I suggest several exercises for them to expand their symbolic systems. Two of my favorite exercises are "Word Association" and "Giving Of Gifts".

Word Association

Word Association is a versatile technique developed by Carl Jung in order to interpret our environment. Dream interpretation and therapy, individual therapy, internal dialogue, and play therapy with children are just some of its applications. Understanding our symbols is instrumental in understanding what we attract and create in our lives. Take the following scenario for example:

I've been having a hard time with my boss. I've had some suggestions that I've wanted to bring up and communicate, but he will not listen to me. I feel ignored and discounted.

Using word association, I can list each of the events and characters, writing down the first association that occurs to me...

"Boss = authority figure", "Talking = expressing myself",
"Suggestions = my own perceptions of self-worth"

Retelling the story, but with my associations, I can apply my situation at work on a more personal level, one that reflects my own thoughts and feelings.

"I've been having a hard time with an authority figure. I can't express myself effectively. And my self worth is being ignored."

Owning The Situation

Processing it further, we can come up with a specific limiting thought or belief; what some people may call a "personal law" or "core belief". We do not wish to project blame by saying, "Authority figures discount me and don't listen." Nor do we wish to degrade ourselves by stating, "I can't communicate to authority figures." Rather, we wish to take full response-ability for the situation without blaming ourselves and/or others. The personal law may take one or more of the following forms:

"I do not feel listened to by authority figures."
"I have a hard time communicating with authority figures."
"I have not acknowledged my own authority."
"I feel my perceptions are discounted by authority figures."

We have now used the environment and its symbology to gain awareness of our own limiting beliefs. With practice, we can take any situation in our lives (a process, dilemma, vision or dream) and interpret it by using the word association technique. Try it yourself:

1) Come up with the opposites of the following cue words. Use the first word that comes to mind. For example: Black = White, Up = Down, etc. If you have a hard time with this, try saying the cue word to yourself while you take a deep breath. On the outbreath, allow the Lower Self to give you the opposite.

Over = ____, High = ____, Pain = ____, Friend = ____,
Running = ____, Mother = ____, Love = ____, New = ____,
Play = ____, Child = ____, The Same = ____, Man = ____

2) Now come up with associations rather than opposites using the following words. For example: Black = Hole, Up = Sky, etc.
Chocolate = ____, Paint = ____, Clothing = ____, Bath = ____,
Ocean = ____, Window = ____, Television = ____, Hands = ____,
Trains = ____, Tunnel = ____, Eagle = ____, Breakfast = ____,

Hammer = ____, Dolphin = ____, Sled = ____, Digging = ___, Hiking = ____, Mountain = ____

3) Now, use the following list of names to come up with additional associations. Just one or two characteristics for each name is enough, but you can come up with more if they occur to you. For example: Father = Dead, Father = Strong, Wife = Caring, Wife = Reliable.

Father = ____, Father = ____, Mother = ____, Mother = ____, Children = ___, Children = ___, Employee = ___, Employee = ____, Grandfather = ____, Grandfather = ____

4) Finally, come up with a string of associations for each of the categories below. Stay open to those associations that have an emotional quality to them. You may get a personal meaning after just one association, or you may need to process several to get to one that does have a feeling attached to it. For example: Employer = Jack, Jack = Efficient, Efficient = Judgements about my efficiency, Judgements about my efficiency = Feeling angry with myself. Now, try it yourself. Add your own personal favorites to this list if you choose.

Employer = ____ = ____ = ____ = ____.
Sister = ____ = ____ = ____ = ____.
Rival = ____ = ____ = ____ = ____.
Enemy = ____ = ____ = ____ = ____.
Friend = ____ = ____ = ____ = ____.
Lover = ____ = ____ = ____ = ____.
Car = ____ = ____ = ____ = ____.
Red = ____ = ____ = ____ = ____.
Moving = ____ = ____ = ____ = ____.
Fishing = ____ = ____ = ____ = ____.
Number "1" = ____ = ____ = ____ = ____.
Eating = ____ = ____ = ____ = ____.
Resting = ____ = ____ = ____ = ____.

It is important to note that our thoughts and feelings are constantly changing! The intellectual and emotional content of our lives is always in flux. The characteristics I associate with one subject today may not be the same characteristics I associate with that same subject next month, next week, or even tomorrow.

Colors And Numbers

Some symbols commonly used by the Lower Self when manifesting and interpreting the environment are colors and numbers. These symbols are rather simple to explore and work with.

Colors show up constantly when exploring one's symbolic system. Colors surround us. They are an important aspect in life. They can be found in dreams, within the Aura or body's energy fields and within the environment (our clothing, food, home decor, etc.). Each color has a certain characteristic associated with it and can reflect and/or evoke specific feelings.

Numbers show up constantly within our lives as well: addresses, phone numbers, birthdates, messages in dreams and visions, and so on. Numerology, the study of numbers, is based on the concept that all numbers have certain inherent meanings and characteristics associated with them.

By studying the meanings and characteristics of colors and numbers we can gain valuable insight. If a certain color, number or set of numbers stands out in our lives or has importance around us, perhaps it is reflecting a personal thought pattern. It may be giving us something we need in order to create balance in our environment.

Coming up with your own interpretations of colors and numbers is a reliable way of creating a personal, understandable communication system. However, there are times when you may wish to rely on "standard" interpretations. You can then see if these standardized associations fit with your own, and cultivate a system that feels right for you.

Colors and numbers are symbolic systems. Some systems are similar and commonly accepted, relating to Jung's Collective Unconscious. Yet, other models are personal and may differ from one individual to another, relating to the Personal Unconscious. How we combine the collective and the personal, how we interpret our environment, dreams and visions, and how we apply these interpretations within our lives is always on an individual basis.

There are many texts on these subjects. However, if you've read more than one treatise on either of these subjects you've probably noticed that there are discrepancies and differences of opinion regarding the interpretations and uses of these various symbols. Of course I'M the one who's right about everything that's contained within *this* text. But then, you're right too if you have your own interpretations.

Many resources are available for the purpose of exploring personal and collective mythologies and symbolic systems. A partial list of these resources is provided at the end of this text. For now, though, please refer to the color and number charts found in the Appendices.

Expanding Intuition

Having become comfortable with the word association technique (and having at least glanced at the color and number charts), it is time to trust your intuition more, and to expand your ability to interpret a wider range of symbols. You can then get feedback on that intuitive sense, trusting and expanding it even more. Two simple exercises for this purpose (taught by one of my teachers, David Starr), are the "Giving of Gifts" and the "House Reading." I have improvised each according to need.

Giving of Gifts

The Guidance meditation previously discussed is an example of the "giving of gifts" exercise. During that exercise we asked Guidance for three gifts we could use at this particular time in our lives. Suppose we had been given a pink elephant as one of the gifts? What would the pink symbolize to us, and what meaning could we attribute to an elephant?

In *my* symbolic system the color pink represents a loving and healing energy, while an elephant represents memory. Putting the two together, I could say that the gift represents a need to recall memories of loving and healing in my life.

As another example, let's use the scenario previously discussed concerning employment. I am having a hard time communicating with my boss. He will not listen to any of my suggestions. Yet I continue trying to convince him of the rightness of my position. I push him to accept my viewpoint. During meditation, my Guidance gives me a "blue bowtie". At face value this is ridiculous!

However, to me, blue represents peace, while a bowtie, being connected to the throat, the communication center of the body, represents talking with others. Hence, the blue bowtie represents a need on my part to communicate more peacefulness. I could apply this gift to my relationship by communicating my viewpoint with more peace. I could also stop the fight by accepting my own perceptions as well as those belonging to my boss. When physically talking with my boss, I could even take a deep breath and remember (symbolically "put on") my blue bowtie.

These gifts may be considered "power objects" in our lives. They are objects that hold certain meaning for us. We can borrow strength and comfort from these objects. We can use them to remind us of something we already have.

Now try this exercise...

The Giving of Gifts Exercise

Pair off with a friend or acquaintance. If in a class situation, pair off with someone you don't know. Designate a "Person A" and a "Person B" within the pair. Sit facing one another and take a couple of centering breaths. Affirm that you are here to learn, to share, and to help one another. Center, call in the Light, affirm your intention to heal and be healed.

Person A: close your eyes and ask that you may give your partner a gift, something that he or she may need or that would be of use in his or her life. Taking a deep breath, reach into an imaginary magic treasure chest located on your lap. On the outbreath, pull out a gift.

Remember that the gift comes from the Lower Self. It is symbolic, so therefore may be rather outlandish, even silly. Don't judge it! The Lower Self is trying to communicate in picture form.

Person A will say to Person B, "I give you ___ which means to me ___." or say, "I give you ___ which could mean ___, or it could mean ___." Just fill in the blanks. You could keep going with "possible" meanings and interpretations until you hit upon one that feels right. Then share that feeling.

Since you are saying the gift means this "to me" or it "could" mean this or that, you CANNOT be wrong. The meaning is based on YOUR personal symbolic system. If you have a hard time interpreting the gift, take a deep breath and say one of the phrases again, this time faster. Again, try to fill in the blank. If you're still having a hard time getting an interpretation, reach into your magic treasure chest and pull out a second gift, one that will help to interpret the first.

I stress the point that you CANNOT do this exercise wrong. If Person A still does not get an interpretation, that is okay. Perhaps it is a symbol that means something to Person B, the person receiving the gift. Or perhaps it is not right at the present time to get an interpretation, and Person B may need to look at his or her own life to see where the gift applies.

If you are having a hard time getting any gift at all from the magic treasure chest, take an imaginary walk through your own home. Look around, see what is on the tables, or hanging on the walls. Say to yourself, "If there is one thing I would give this person what would that be?" Give Person B the gift, and interpret it as you would a gift from the treasure chest. Give a total of three gifts.

Get some feedback (avoid criticism!) from the receiver of the gifts. What does that gift mean to the receiver? How can it be applied to his or her life? Person B: thank Person A for the gift, even if you have no idea what it means. Person A: thank your Lower Self for connecting with the other person, and for sharing. When this is done, switch. Person B be the giver, and person A the receiver.

When all is said and done, thank your partner. A hug may be appropriate. Remember, it's a lot easier to get a hug if you give one.

- - -

If this exercise is difficult at first, I encourage you to stick with it. Perhaps the receiver, the person being "read" was hard to read. Maybe you were too emotionally involved with your partner, and some of your own feelings got in the way. Perhaps your desire to understand on a "logical" level prevented you from letting your intuition have free reign.

To make this exercise easier and less threatening, you can practice it independently. Next time you're out and about, at a mall, stopped at a red light, or just walking along, focus on a stranger, take a deep breath and do the exercise silently. This gives "people watching" a whole new dimension! Next time you're concerned about someone, tune in and mentally give him or her a gift complete with interpretation. Affirm you intent to grow, to learn, and to heal. Give yourself a gift, perhaps a new way of helping that person within the worrisome situation.

If you are still have a difficult time with this process, you may wish to simply drop it for a while and get back to it later. For example, some time ago I had been studying a certain symbolic system. I studied it long and hard but could not use the system effectively. It just wouldn't come naturally, so I gave up. Several months later, while giving someone a reading, I found myself relying solely upon that symbolic system. Afterward, it was easily accessible.

Sometimes it just takes time for those symbols to "sink in", to be accepted into one's own personal mythology. Be patient while integrating these symbols more personally.

The House Reading

And Psyche, after returning form the Underworld, did acknowledge her own beauty. Having attracted the attention of Eros, the God of Love, she was then taken to the Upperworld. And she met her destiny.

This exercise, the House Reading, is slightly more challenging than the Giving of Gifts, but by now you're up to the task. Being more in depth and having more versatility, this exercise may be used as a spring board for integrating any number of symbols.

As with the Giving of Gifts, pair off with a partner. Being the person designated as the "reader", close your eyes and take a few deep centering breaths. Affirm that you are here to learn and share, and to help one another. Focus on the Highest Good by surrounding yourself and your partner with the White Light. Now ask yourself to see your partner's SYMBOLIC house. This represents his or her life, how she expresses herself and interacts with her environment. Your partner can even take notes as you are doing the reading.

What does her front door look like? (How does she let people into her life?) Is the door big or small, open or closed, easy or hard to open, locked to the hilt or easily accessible? Is it well lit or dark and gloomy? When you get the picture and relate it to your partner remember to say, "It could mean ___" or "To me this means ___." This gives you permission to be wrong, as well as right. It also gives your partner permission to relate the symbols to her own life, to interpret the pictures personally and perhaps more thoroughly.

After going through the door and into the house, look around. What does the living room look like? (How does your partner accept others into her life once she has let them in? How does she entertain them? What part of herself does she show other people?) How much space is there? What kind of furniture is present? Try looking out the front window. (How does your partner view her world?) Now look at your feet. What is the floor like–hard, soft, wood, carpet, colored, plain, dirt? (How does she connect with the physical and material world?) Are there any pictures on the walls? How's the lighting? Is there anything else you may need to be aware of before moving on?

Now let's go into the kitchen and dining room area. (How does your partner nurture herself and those around her?) What does the table look like? How many chairs are around the table? Is the table set? What does the floor look like? Check out the stove. Is it clean or dirty? Is there anything on the "back burner", and how long has it been there? And now for the refrigerator. Is there foodstuff in there? How much? Is it fresh or old and moldy?

Look out the back door. (What are your partner's personal concerns, hobbies or private interests?) How easy or hard does that door open? (Don't go out there unless invited.) Is there anything else you need to pay attention to before moving on?

Now ask yourself to see the way downstairs. (We are now going down to the person's Lower Self.) How do you access it-a stairway, elevator, pole or something else? On your way down, look around. What is it like? (How easy is it for your partner to contact her Lower Self?) Is it well lit, narrow, wide, easy or dangerous? Is it clean and well used or musty with spiders?

Once in the basement, look around. Is there a study? Are there games? Is it a family room or a storage room? Are there laundry facilities? Is the basement clean or messy? What is one thing your partner may get rid of? Is there anything down there that your partner may have use of in the main part of the house? Is there anything else you may need to see before exiting the basement?

While coming back upstairs, be aware of anything important. Is it hard or easy? How do you feel? (How does she listen to her Lower Self?)

Okay. It's time. Check out your partner's bathroom where she "cleans up her act" and lets go of stuff no longer needed. It is also the place in which we get ourselves ready to meet with other people-to put on our "face". Where is the bathroom located? Is there one on the main level? If not, is there one upstairs? If so, then find your way upstairs.

The access to the higher level is the connection with the Higher Self. Is there a staircase? If so, how wide, how steep? Is it safe or dangerous, used or unused? Are there any turns in the staircase? If so, after how many steps? Is there an elevator? What is that like? Are there any colors that stand out in your mind? As you continue on your way upstairs, look around. Feel what it's like. Is it easy or hard?

Enter the bathroom. Is it large and spacious or crowded and difficult to access? What does the sink look like? Is there a mirror, how big? Look into the mirror. What do you see? (How does your partner see herself?) How about the shower or tub area? Do any colors stand out anywhere in the bathroom?

The toilet! Oh, NO! Not the toilet! Is it clean or dirty? Sit on it. What do you see around you? (What is your partner releasing?) How hard or easy is it to get up? Look around. Is there anything else of importance before you leave that space?

If you haven't gone upstairs yet, do so now. Be aware of the process. Continue your journey, going to the bedroom. What is the door like? (How does your partner find her way to that place of rest?). After opening the door, look around. What color is the room? (How easily does your partner rest, leaving the everyday world and connecting with Spirit-beyond or past the physical body?) Is it comfortable? Is the bed simple or ornate? (Does she connect with Spirit simply or through ritual?) Are there any mirrors? How many? (Can your partner look at herself and her Spiritual nature easily? How does she view that part of herself?)

Lie on the bed and look up. What does the ceiling look like? (What does she focus on when connecting with Spirit?) What color is the ceiling? Are there posters or pictures, a skylight perhaps? Is there anything else that calls your attention right now?

Is it easy or hard to get off the bed? What is the feeling? (How does she leave the realm of Spirit and prepare herself for the everyday world?) Take a look at the dresser(s) and closet. (How does she take off her coverings, her clothing, her masks or roles in life?) Is her clothing easily accessible? How many choices does she have? Is the bedroom set up for more than one person? How does that feel?

Is there anything else you may need to look at before you exit the bedroom? Is there a gift you would like to leave for that person? If so, leave it somewhere noticeable and readily available.

Upon leaving the bedroom, go back downstairs, noticing everything and anything of importance. (How does your partner integrate Spirit into her life?) Is there anything else in the house that calls your attention? Make a note of it.

Mentally thank your partner for letting you into her space. And look for the exit. How easy or hard is it to leave? (How does your partner let go of people in her life?) Assure your partner that if it's right to connect with her in the future, you will do so. Thank her and leave, closing the door behind you if it was closed before.

When you are complete with the exercise, ask for feedback. Explore any symbols that did not have an interpretation attached to them. Your partner may have an interpretation. The symbol may have been drawn from HER symbolic system, not yours.

We manifest those symbols that are of importance to us.

There may be a wonderful little twist here. Because we all manifest things in our lives that symbolize our wants and needs, you may find yourself picking up on parts of that person's ACTUAL house. This is natural. And what a wonderful surprise for both of you if you do pick up on tangibly "real" objects and descriptions.

When I first started learning how to give "psychic readings" I would often do this exercise along with the Giving of Gifts. One time I gave my partner a motorcycle which, to me, represented freedom. My partner's mouth dropped wide open. She shared with me that the maintenance and gas expense of her old car was getting to be too much so she went out the previous week and bought a motorcycle! She had wanted the freedom that a motorcycle gave her.

I was shocked as well, realizing that, not only had I given her this "symbolic" gift, but she had already manifested it within her life. Associating motorcycles with freedom very strongly, she wanted this reflected within her environment. In yet another reading, I picked up on a house that my partner had just bought. Symbols are wonderful! They are everywhere. We interpret, process, and manifest them all the time.

The Treasure Map

The use of symbols is not limited to interpreting. We can also use those symbols to change our thoughts and to manifest a more positive environment. We can "change the dream".[25]

The treasure map is a wonderful tool that can be used for focus and manifestation. It is a collection of pictures, drawings and possibly statements representing what we want in our lives. We pick things that symbolize what we wish to manifest (how we wish our external dream to be), and put them on paper. We can glue them, tape, staple or draw them. I saw one Treasure Map in which the person made a mobile and hung it from the ceiling. We can use whatever form is pleasurable.

With our goals on paper we have something to focus on. The goals become more tangible. The pictures become Visual Affirmations, and our thoughts have more power. In the previous example, expressing myself to my boss, I might choose a picture of an authority figure in my life. I would then put a picture of myself right beside it, at the same level, symbolizing equality. A pink bowtie might also be nice.

Remember the car story? While trying to manifest the perfect means of transportation, I, at one point, hung a bumper sticker on my bedroom wall. I talked to the universe, "There's part of my car. Now let's have the rest!" Amazingly, the car I received had the same bumper sticker!

I also like to put a verbal affirmation at the bottom or top of my Treasure Map, "This or something better is now manifesting for me, in the perfect form, and for the Highest Good of myself and all concerned."[26] In this way I affirm the manifestation process as taking place in the present moment rather than in the future. I bless my present circumstances and extend those blessings toward the future. I also remove any limitations regarding form and any fear of negative consequences.

Some people make big Treasure Maps and hang them in a central location. I prefer to make a small one and place it in the beginning of my appointment calendar. Wherever you choose to put yours, make sure it is someplace that will present itself to you often.

We automatically do word association all the time.

We always use our personal mythology to create things within our lives. It's wonderful, though, to use the process consciously for understanding, growth and positive change.

We see a person, place or thing within the environment and then interpret it. We assign associations and interpretations to that event and act accordingly, manifesting another event which symbolizes our associations and interpretations.

The symbolic process resembles the Rational Emotive Therapy (RET) Model presented earlier. If the outcome is positive, we can simply affirm it and thank ourselves for manifesting something positive. However, if the outcome is limiting, we can challenge the thoughts and feelings, the "personal law" or "core belief" that created the limitation. By conscious choice, we can then manifest more positive beliefs in the environment.

For example, let's use the employment situation once again. The personal law or core belief I came up with was one of the following:

"I do not feel listened to by authority figures."
"I have a hard time communicating with authority figures."
"I have not acknowledged my own authority."
"My perceptions are discounted by authority figures."

After discovering one or more personal laws, we can journal, developing positive thoughts to challenge the limiting beliefs. In the future, when confronted with a similar situation, we can take a deep, centering breath, ground and/or call in the Light, verbally and visually remind ourselves of the positive thoughts, and change the dream...

"I acknowledge my own self worth."
"I accept my self as the authority figure in my life."
"I communicate more safely, easily and lovingly with everyone around me."
"I remember, even feel, my blue bowtie."

Regardless of the type of symbol we manifest within our physical environment, we relate our thoughts and feelings to it. Then, we have a choice: manifest the same pattern or create something new.

First Choice: Manifest The Same Outcome

(A)	(B)	(C)		
Activating Event	Belief	Emotional Consequence	Action	Outcome
-	-	-		
Offering Suggestions	Having Hard Time With Authority	Sadness Anger Tension	Ineffectual Communication	Not Listened to

Second Choice: Challenge The Old, Create The New

(A)	(B)	(C)		
Activating Event	Belief	Emotional Consequence	Action	Outcome
-	-	-		
Offering Suggestions	Accepting Self-Worth, Authority	Relaxation Self-Assurance	Effective Communication	Being Listened to!

This, however, is not a one time affair. We manifest something, interpret the environment, reprogram the thoughts and symbols, manifest, interpret, reprogram and so on. It is endless.

Additionally, by bringing the thoughts to a more personal level, we learn lessons, clear relationships, and apply the positive thoughts to other areas of our lives as well. In the above example regarding the employer or "authority figure", we did not merely affirm that "my employer is listening to me". We reprogrammed the thoughts ABOVE the specific level of just ONE person, applied it to self and therefore to EVERYONE around us. We owned the situation and resolved it by "accepting our own self-worth and authority", creating ramifications THROUGHOUT our lives. Taking the process above the physical level, we allow change to happen EVERYWHERE within our lives–past memories, present situations and future outcomes.

Please see the following diagram for a summary of this process.

The Process: Taking It Above The Physical Level
(follow steps 1 through 7)

- 4 -
Focus on a
positive thought and symbol.

- 3 - Explore the limiting thought.	- 5 - Affirm the positive thought.
- 2 - Interpret the symbology.	- 6 - Affirm the positive symbol.
- 1 - See the Environment.	- 7 - Wait and watch the results.

- - -

The journey to self awareness is knowledge, wisdom, and manifestation.

- - -

- 9 -

Exploring the Past: The Challenge

...and then he said she felt I wanted what he wanted, but I said he felt he asked for what she said he wanted...Of this, I am certain!

The Lower Self assigns values or beliefs to certain symbols (specific events) according to past experience. It has learned to deal with certain situations through experience, repetition and the voice of authority.[27]

Experience and Tangibility

EXPERIENCE refers to something being real enough if it has enough validity and face value. If we can sense, see, taste, hear and feel it, it is TANGIBLE. We then accept it as real, putting our belief and energy into it. Additionally, if we attach a lot of emotional energy to a certain experience, that experience becomes more firmly rooted or anchored within our belief system, more tangible. With more tangibility and validity, however, comes more emotional energy, then more validity, more emotional attachment, and so on. These two team up to form memories.

For example, many of us, when growing up, were yelled at when our parents were angry. With the increased emotional charge (our parents' and our own) we may tend to remember those times more than the times that were without the high emotional intensity. Given ten loving experiences and only one angry one, if the loving experiences were not accompanied by great emotion, we will tend to remember the one angry situation more.

Loving experiences are best remembered when experienced with high emotional intensity.

Wouldn't it be wonderful if our parents whispered to us when they were angry and YELLED at us when they were loving! One therapeutic tool I experienced, the Celebration Shout, involved just that. The assembled group arranged themselves in lines. The leader blew a whistle, whereupon the first person in each line ran up front, turned around and faced the others in line. That person then yelled at the top of his lungs that he loved himself, and yelled all the reasons for being lovable, loved and perfect. Everyone else also yelled, encouraging and urging him onward, affirming his positive traits. When the leader blew the whistle again, the person in front ran to the end of the line, and the next person in line presented himself to the group. This process continued until everyone had at least one turn in front. What a wonderful ritual in making our love tangible! I'll remember it for the rest of my life.

The celebration shout is but one ritual. Yet, there are rituals virtually everywhere, in every religion, in every home. They are used to provide tangible, personal experiences that the Lower Self will pay attention to. Even though the Lower Self KNOWS it is participating in a ritual, it still uses the ritual as it would any memory. Ritual makes the healing experience TANGIBLE.

Repetition

With REPETITION, we remember an experience, and we expect the same outcome or something similar to manifest itself in the future. The more we experience something with all our senses, the more real it seems to be. And this works more effectively when we attach emotional energy to those experiences.

Those experiences, however, include the negative, painful, sad and limiting beliefs, as well as the positive ones. If the beliefs are positive, all the more power to them. But if they limit us in one way or another, then we now have a wonderful opportunity to repeatedly challenge them. Just being aware of a limiting thought when it arises can go a long way in changing old patterns. With awareness, we can then say to ourselves: "Wait a second. Things can be different now. They do NOT have to be the same as in the past."

The Voice of Authority

The VOICE OF AUTHORITY refers to that person or entity who we listen to and endow with importance. While growing up, the voice of authority may have been our parents as they laid down the rules. It may have been a teacher, religious leader, or politician. The voice of authority may even be called "Mass Consciousness"–the rules set down by society in general. However, in challenging our old belief systems, we can change the voice of authority from an external source (eg. parents, teachers) to an internal source. In Gestalt therapy this is called owning our own feelings, making ourselves the "Locus of Control" within our environment. We are the ones response-able for our feelings, beliefs and actions.

This does not mean that we have the right to tell others what THEY should believe. But rather, we can share our beliefs, and allow others to accept or reject them as they will. We can take control of our own lives without taking control of others'. Sure, how we think and act does have an impact on others, but it is egocentric to think that we can control others. We are the authority in our lives, and others are the authority in their lives. In this way we learn to love, respect and empower ourselves at the same time we learn to love, respect and empower others.

This is where self-talk and being aware of our own thought structures plays a very important role. Knowing how we set certain patterns into motion and deciding which thoughts are holding us back, we can then proceed to change them. We can go for the Highest thoughts possible.

We become the Voice of Authority and remove limitations from the past by identifying with what we feel to be our maximum potential, our highest aspirations, our Soul's path in life.

Dialogue Between the Middle and Lower Selves

Working out of my Middle Self, I try to figure out and deduce the causes of past or present events within my environment. I then, based on perceived consequences, induce changes in my actions and within the environment. Referring to a theory of personality, Behaviorism, this type of behavior resembles "Operant Conditioning". A person will DEDUCE patterns from the environment, and then act in ways to INDUCE a change in or to "operate upon" that environment.

This Deductive and Inductive Reasoning of the Middle Self is rather amazing; looking at the past, projecting into the future, sorting, filing, deducing, deciding, and inducing change. If A = B, and B = C, then A = C and so on. The Middle Self, with its blueprints, data systems and drawing boards is always seeking ways to affect the environment.

The Lower Self, on the other hand, has quite different processes. Its reasoning abilities and approaches to things differ dramatically from those of the Middle Self. Wherein the Middle Self works out of Operant Conditioning, Deductive and Inductive Reasoning, the Lower Self works out of Classical Conditioning, its reasoning being Deductive and Associative. "The Low Self thinks deductively, but is unable to reason inductively as the Middle Self does."[28] The Lower Self interprets the environment according to its beliefs, but does not act directly to change those beliefs.

When confronted with new experiences, the Lower Self can be likened to a blank drawing board. In Classical Conditioning, when presented with two sets of stimuli, the subject associates those two stimuli as belonging together. It doesn't matter if it makes sense to us or not; if two things belong together, they belong together. As a child, perhaps my family got a new car and then moved. Consequently, I had to leave my friends and became lonely. My Lower Self, having associated these experiences with one another, concluded that getting a car EQUALS moving EQUALS being lonely. $A = A = A = A$ and so on. The Lower Self draws from past experience, adds emotional significance and associations, and comes up with an interpretation, a rule of thumb, a personal law or core belief. This constantly repeating "tape" is brought into adulthood, often staying hidden from the Middle Self's awareness unless something or someone brings it to light.

As we grow older, the Middle Self may have more control, but the Lower Self still has considerable power. The child within us does not grow up; it remains a child. The Lower Self still follows learned rules from years ago, relying on the past in order to interpret the present. It does not necessarily look for alternative ways of responding to stimuli. It cannot, in and of itself, induce a change in its own belief system. For that it needs outside input: different experiences and/or input from the Middle Self. Without the Middle Self's help in "re-associating" cause and effect, the Lower Self continues to transmit its undisputed beliefs to the Higher Self. Its old associations manifest themselves over and over again, creating the same or similar events.

To illustrate this process more clearly I'd like to share my "Bicycle Story". I don't think it's based on my own past experience, but since I've been telling this same story over and over again for many years, I'm beginning to have my doubts. Maybe it really did happen.

Bicycle Story

Pretend you're a child getting your first bicycle. It's a wonderful experience and in your excitement, while riding it, you crash into your dad's car. He gets angry and makes you do extra chores in order to help pay for repairs. You have more work, less money, less play time, and hurt feelings. To top it off, you also twisted your ankle, so you're limping your way through this disaster.

With the Lower Self's associative reasoning, everything experienced around this event becomes grouped together into what we may call an emotional cluster. L. Ron Hubbard, "originator" of Dianetics, calls this cluster an "engram", the total experience being imprinted within the body on a cellular level. All the thoughts and emotions connected with a particular situation tend to cluster around one another. The "A = A = A" dynamic takes hold:

A	=	A	=	A	=	A	=	A	=	A
Bike		Accident		Anger from authority figure		Work		Less Money		Hurt Ankle

Now for the exciting part: it's thirty years later and you want to get a bicycle. Oh No! The Lower Self may not wish to face the emotional and physical pain from the first incident. You may create other expenses, thus preventing the purchase of a bicycle. You may create a physical ailment to prevent riding a bicycle, or perhaps you'll simply "decide" that you really don't want a bicycle.

You may get that bike, and as you're riding in street traffic, you're so worried about getting into an accident that, looking over your shoulder, you run head-on into something. All of a sudden A = A, bike = accident. Riding the bike, you may get to work late one or more times and suddenly A = A, bike = authority figure (boss) being angry at you. You may get docked pay at work or perhaps need to put in over time.

All of a sudden A = A = A, bike = accident = authority figure being angry = more work = less money (especially if you need to fix the bike). In an extreme, you may even experience pain from the old foot injury, or you may re-injure that same foot, A = A, bike = hurt foot. You may even hurt your foot badly, or ruin the bicycle so completely that you cannot ride the bike. The conflict has now been effectively resolved, but not in a healthy or happy way.

So far, the initial incident and subsequent incident thirty years later are extremely similar. However, now some additional things may happen just to make life a little more interesting. After the boss docks your pay at work you may get angry at him or her. Another "A" has now been added: Getting angry AT an authority figure, whereas previously we had received anger FROM an authority figure. Working late to make up for lost time or to save money in order to fix the bike, you may even miss a few evenings out with friends. What a mess!

From our first experience we have:

Bike = Accident = Anger = Work = Less = Hurt
                  from   Money   Ankle
              authority figure

To which we add our second experience:

Anger AT   =   Separation from
Authority Figures   friends, loneliness

Suddenly the original emotional cluster has gained a new dimension, additional associations! The two separate incidents are no longer separate. Memories and emotional charge from one may bring up memories and emotional charge from the other. Resistance increases when trying to manifest that bike and/or when trying to maintain your lifestyle after getting the bike.

The response to that resistance may vary from one individual to the next: (1) We can let go of getting a bike. (2) We can push through and get a bike despite the resistance. (3) We can put up with the negative consequences after getting the bike, or (4) We can dialogue and release the resistance.

I recommend dialogue-looking at our manifestations, interpreting the symbols presented to us, and challenging any limiting thoughts that we discover. In this way we can reprogram the limiting thoughts and manifest more positive ones within our life. Being aware of our limitations, we can deal with them consciously, instead of being controlled by our past choices. And what about other issues in our life such as finding a loving partner, managing money, or engaging in successful activities? The Lower Self has a voice in all of these, and the time to open friendly dialogue is now!

The Lower Self As Child

Imagine a child who wants something. He tries talking with you, but you are too busy to pay attention. What does that child do? Speaks more loudly, of course! If that child is still ignored, he might start screaming! If necessary, he could get your attention by acting out.

The Lower Self has that same need to express itself and to act upon its memories. If not listened to, it will communicate its feelings and beliefs more loudly to whoever will listen. The Higher Self, our Creative Force is ALWAYS listening. If we ignore the Lower Self in the short run, we spend a lot more time in the future dealing with its issues and resulting manifestations. However, spending time in the short run - giving the Lower Self attention and love, changing those past memories and beliefs - we can prevent trouble now rather than chasing it down later.

When listening to the Lower Self as with a child, we can start by first letting go of any judgments we have about what the Lower Self wishes to communicate. We need to thank the Lower Self for sharing. For if we continue to judge the Lower Self negatively, he may do what any child would do - shut up, and then act out on the side.

Sure, some of the beliefs and feelings of the Lower Self may look like the craziest things that have ever come out of an adult's mind. But, lots of thoughts which seem totally illogical to us are perfectly logical to a child. Albert Ellis (RET) originally called these thoughts "irrational beliefs", but by referring to the Lower Self's beliefs as irrational, we may be automatically judging those thoughts as wrong. They are NOT illogical to the Lower Self. They merely limit our responses to certain situations. Consequently, I prefer to call these beliefs "limiting" or "hindering" rather than illogical.

It is not the emotion in and of itself that is limiting. It is the cause of that emotion, as well as the consequence, that may be limiting.

Have you ever said, or had someone else say to you, "Don't be angry, don't be sad"? That's like saying "Don't feel your feelings." That seems rather limiting because if we do not give ourselves permission to feel our own emotions, we will not know what they are. If we ignore a feeling or judge it as wrong, it does not go away. Instead, it gets tucked into a little corner and sneaks out, creating mischief when we're not looking. Feel your feelings! We don't have a right to hurt others with what we're feeling, but we've got every right to feel what we're feeling.

Albert Ellis, in one of his seminars, stated that we only make matters worse by feeling we shouldn't be angry or sad. We only make matters worse by being angry because we're angry, or sad because we're sad. We do not need that "secondary emotional concern" preventing us from discovering the cause of the primary emotional concern. His favorite phrase during that seminar was "...so you're angry, so you're sad. No big f*** deal! (Now let's deal with what's behind that feeling.)."[29]

Re-Choosing The Pattern

In challenging our limiting thoughts, I recommend dialoguing with the Lower Self on paper, keeping a journal. This needn't be complicated. It can be a simple journal in which the Middle and Lower Selves can communicate. With self-talk, we can discover our limiting beliefs and then offer alternative responses. Instead of merely affirming or ignoring the old tapes, we can challenge and change them. The Lower Self needs new input in order to change the rules. The present Voice of Authority, the Middle Self, can let the Lower Self see that new things are possible. New beliefs CAN manifest in the environment.

Referring to the bicycle story, my journaled dialogue might look like the following.

Middle Self	Lower Self
I want to get a bicycle.	
	But I'm afraid of getting into an accident.
	What if others get angry with me?
It's safe to get a bike.	
It's okay to have that fear, but we CAN get support on this.	
	But I remember the last bike I got. It cost me a whole lot of hard work and money.
Okay. That was past experience, but it can be different now. It doesn't have to cost a lot.	
	Well, I can't afford one now. I should start saving money.
Getting a bike could be effortless, with little or no cost. And we can get one at the perfect time. Let's work on it together.	
	OK, I'll give it a try.
Thank you. I love you.	

The above dialogue is just an example. As you'll remember, my original car story spanned a year's time. However, with practice and patience, journaling can become more effective and have almost immediate results. As we progress in this text, we will experience different methods of journaling. But for now we are just getting a framework in which to explore the environment and ourselves with more self-acceptance and love.

Remember, dialoguing is a process. We may or may not get to a point of total clarity--we may just get clearer on things at deeper and deeper levels. The emotional charges and associations from any previous event may become clustered together with other seemingly separate events. These clusters may also be combined with other ones. There might always be a connecting thought or experience! Everything in one's life is connected with everything else. A = A = A = A ad infinitum.

Even with conscientious and diligent self-talk, we may not clear all the resistance. Stuff slips through! Limiting thoughts and feelings, whichever ones are left, may manifest. Looking at this process, we may go into overwhelm: How can I ever clear these limitations? With so much going on, how can I ever understand my own process, my own conflicting needs and wants? How can I ever change conflict into agreement, creating balance and harmony within my life? And if I take care of one priority, doesn't something else then become a priority? When will the process end? Ever?

At first, this may seem pessimistic. However, once we realize that we may never be totally clear, that we may never know everything, we can let ourselves off the hook for being who we are and for feeling what we're feeling. Everyone's process is unique, and the timing is just as individual. If we were to change completely overnight, many of us may not be able to integrate those changes in our lives anyway–we may revert to old patterns because of the Lower Self's need for safety.

We all have the perfect amount of resistance at all times.

Accepting that we don't have to become aware of and fix everything all at once allows us to forgive ourselves for our limitations, and realize our perfectness now...as is. We can give ourselves a break and make the expectations of ourselves reasonable. By accepting ourselves more as we are, we ironically give ourselves more permission to risk growth and change! With permission to be more aware of our limiting thoughts, we can dialogue, and have a better chance at clarity.

Life then becomes a process, a journey into self discovery. With new input, the old tapes change. With practice, the process becomes easier, more effective, and more loving. We have the power right here and now to create a better life for ourselves and those around us. We can foster an atmosphere of love, respect and cooperation. Having the courage to face our limitations, we can begin to let them go. We can live more fully, more happily, more creatively, now!

We Can Enjoy The Journey.

- - -

- 10 -

The Body as Symbol

And I look upon you, my body, and see that you are my friend. What are you trying to tell me? Speak up if you have to. Let me see. Let me hear. Let me feel. And we will heal one another.

When looking at our environment–past, present or future, we may not always take time to journal. Things are looking kind of rosy. We're on track, meeting our goals. Things are good, so why look at things more deeply? Yet we suddenly may get sick, have an ache or pain, or perhaps an accident. So why did this happen? How can we heal it, and what can we do to prevent a similar dis-ease in the future?

We can ignore a lot of events in our external environment, but when it comes to the body, the internal environment, spending time in ignorance is harder. When something goes wrong, when pain is tangible, we become highly motivated to do something about it.

My personal belief is that all illness is psychological in nature, meaning that my own individual thoughts and feelings influence the state of my physical body. This belief not only helps me take response-ability for my dis-eased state, but it helps me to heal it as well. After all, if I have a hand in generating my own discomfort, then it follows that I also have a hand in creating my own wellness. The concept of owning a dis-ease is not meant to project blame upon myself if I get sick or have a hard time healing myself. Nor does it discount the good work of many health professionals. However, it does give me the feeling that I have a certain amount of control over my body and that I am not helpless or at the mercy of other people, medications, healers and so on.

I cannot truthfully say that there is a definitive line drawn between what we attract or cause to happen to us and what seemingly just happens to us. However, if I make an error in judgment, I prefer it to be on the side of self-response-ability, on having a semblance of control in my life.

When dis-ease is present, I do not know where to drawn the line between what is a purely "physical" cause and what is a result of our psychological nature. Therefore I opt for fanaticism: everything has a mental and emotional basis. At the very least, working with my dis-ease mentally and emotionally can compliment any and all physical therapies I use.

Seeking the advice of a medical practitioner, several if needed, is always advisable. However, the choice of healing methods is ultimately up to the patient. When we are ready to heal ourselves, we will. We will find the right method to do so, or we will find the right person to affect the healing.

In my healing practice, many referrals are from medical practitioners such as doctors, chiropractors and nutritionists. They may feel that the patient's physical condition is not healing "appropriately" due to some possible mental and emotional stressors slowing down the process. I then see the client one or more times and, if necessary, the client continues treatment with the initial healer. After releasing some of the mental and emotional stressors surrounding the dis-ease, the client's other therapy will be more effective, and the dis-ease will not be exacerbated further.

Metaphysiology:
Mental and Emotional Causes of Physical Illness;
Memory Attributes and Symbolic Applications

There are two basic psychological causes of physical illness: memory attributes and symbolic applications. Memory attributes are based on the pain and discomfort from previous experiences of illness or accident. The Lower Self has a vivid blueprint of associations between body, mind, and emotions. Tapping into any one aspect of a memory can easily bring forth whatever the Lower Self has associated with it. Thus, we may have a tendency to re-experience the same dis-ease or to re-injure ourselves in a similar pattern as the Lower Self contributes its input to present situations. For example, let's look at the bicycle story presented earlier. Remember, A = A = A...

Bike = Accident = Anger = Work = Less Money = Hurt Ankle

The hurt ankle is included within this emotional cluster. The Lower Self remembers the whole experience and attributes any and all of its components to each other, including the hurt ankle. The memory of that incident, along with any tension and limiting emotions or fears, are within that ankle. This not only hinders the healing process in the present, but can make the ankle more prone to accident or injury in the future when any component of the emotional cluster gets "triggered".

Additionally, the Lower Self prefers to avoid painful experiences and memories. The Lower Self pulls energy and awareness away from any part of the body that taps into that pain, resulting in less energy, less awareness, and the increased possibility of accident or illness. Thus, a future situation in which the Lower Self feels it has to work harder for less money, for example, can contribute to a newly sprained ankle.

The other aspect of dis-ease, "symbolic application", relates to the symbols the Lower Self applies to various parts of the body. I find it useful in my practice to refer to the term "Metaphysiology". Physiology refers to the study of the function of the body and its parts. Meta means above or beyond. Putting the two together, we study what is above the function of the body and its parts...and this is THOUGHT.

For instance, one of the functions of the legs is to carry us forward in life, to be more independent, helping us to "stand on our own".

Acting on plans, going toward the future, we "put our best foot forward". If the Lower Self has a thought, "it hurts to act (go forward) on something," this one thought alone may contribute to an accident or dis-ease within one or both legs. The Lower Self may feel, "OH, I don't want to go forward on this," or "It hurts to do that." The result is tension and/or lack of awareness in the part of the body that symbolizes going forward, making it more prone to accident or illness.

Have you ever hurt the same part of your body repeatedly? Probably! Why do you hurt one part of your body instead of another? One day you stub your big toe. Later that same day someone steps on it. The next day you drop something and, wouldn't you know it, it lands on that same toe! Or perhaps you hit the same elbow several times in as many days. This could be a result of symbolism relating to the body. Maybe we don't have enough "elbow room" in order to express ourselves. Perhaps we really don't want to put some "elbow grease" into something.

Through symbolic application, one part of the body becomes more prone to illness than another based upon the limiting thoughts and fears associated with it. A resulting illness then becomes a part of memory, which in turn strengthens and affirms the symbolism we already associate with that body part. Anticipating pain and wanting to avoid it, the Lower Self then draws energy and awareness away from that body part. This is now clearly an invitation for doors, chairs and other people to just reach out and hit, crush or mash it. That part of the body has now become an accident just waiting to happen.

Interestingly enough, if we DO injure a part of the body, we will naturally be "forced" to focus more attention on it. We will wish to heal it. Yet, to help heal it effectively, we can put our attention on not only the physical healing process, but also on the emotional and mental processes. Releasing the limiting memories and tension associated with the body and its symbolic function, we can heal faster. We can rid ourselves of the past physical dis-ease, AND the tendency to re-injure it in the future. A tree that bends in the wind does not break. Getting more awareness and positive energy into the body, it then has a better chance of healing itself.

Metaphysiology can be applied to any and all parts of the body. We can start the healing process by exploring the personal symbolism attached to a body part. We can then explore any memories attached to that symbolism. For instance, the back functions to give us support. The part of the back closest to the Earth supports much of the weight of the body. Therefore, the lower back addresses our needs, wants, and fears related to our physical, material support. If someone around us is sick, we may fear illness ourselves. We become acutely aware of our own mortality, creating tension within the body, specifically, the lower back. A change in jobs, living situations, expenses, or anything that threatens our sense of security and physical/material well-being can have the same effect and be felt in the lower back.

As a further example, the middle of the back (closest to our heart) relates to emotional support, the level of acceptance we have for ourselves and/or others. Do we "stab ourselves in the back" because of guilt, or do we "pat ourselves on the back" for our accomplishments?

The upper back, closest to our shoulders, relates to the support we receive from and give to others. Do we get enough support? Do we give enough? Are we "shouldering too much of a burden," or not enough?

When faced with any physical accident or dis-ease, the first step in the healing process (in addition to healing it physically) is to see what that body part is used for. What is its symbolic function?

Then we can address memories associated with that part of the body as well as its symbolism. Did we injure that body part previously? If so, what was going on in our lives at that point in time? Is there something similar going on now? After answering these questions, we can see if there is a limiting thought or feeling we have applied to our environment and/or body.

With an understanding of the interplay between memory attributes and symbolic applications, we now have a new tool to guide us in our healing. We can learn the body's language, dialogue with it, and release the thought or feeling through therapy, journaling, imagery or action. We can redirect our energies toward a healthier, limitless future.

Polarity Therapy

As an additional guide, we may look at the concept of polarity therapy, relating to the electromagnetic charges within the body and how they are reflected in mental/emotional issues.

Generally, the left side of the body is negative in electromagnetic charge, while the right side is positive. The left side of the body is feminine in nature, while the right side is masculine. The feminine qualities include nurturing, patience, caring, emotionality, Spiritual energies, passivity, taking energy inward. The masculine qualities include dominance, impatience, the urge toward action, attention on the physical world, aggressiveness, putting energy outward.

The left leg carries us forward on emotional concerns and personal relationships, while the right leg allows us to act upon physical, material concerns and any decisions. The left hand and arm receive support (emotional AND financial), while the right gives support. The left shoulder relates to our perceived "response-ability" to receive support, while the right refers to the response-ability to give support.

Polarity therapy involves both hands-on healing and counseling. The hands-on healing helps the body to connect the positive and negative electrical charges within the body. The counseling aspect helps to connect the masculine and feminine parts of our psyche so they can cooperate with, rather than antagonize, each other.

We can even relate this to neuro-psychology, in that the right side of the brain generally controls the left side of the body, and the left brain controls the right side of the body. Through polarity therapy we help the two sides of the body communicate with each other, we help integrate our masculine and feminine energies, and we may actually be helping to integrate the two hemispheres of the brain.

Specific Symbology

When exploring internal organs and systems, we can look closely at the functions involved–both the expected, normal functions, as well as any that may be inhibited by dis-ease. In this context, we can look at the physical cause-and-effect of the physical ailment, and then the functional cause-and-effect. We can then apply the results, on a symbolic level, to our mental and emotional states.

For instance, on a physical level the kidneys filter our blood, functioning to help the body keep what it needs and let go of what it does not. Are we having a hard time deciding which of our own feelings we need to keep, and which ones we need to release? Perhaps some sadness or anger is useful when deciding what we need and want because it motivates us to act. "Should" we hold on to those feelings? Any imbalance, judgments, or fears about retaining or releasing feelings may be reflected in the kidneys. Similar issues having to do with holding-on or letting go could also effect the colon (constipation/diarrhea) and/or the hands. These seemingly unrelated physical body parts actually have some common meta-physical functions.

We use the same language associated with the body as a metaphor applied to the psyche. In exploring symbolic applications of the body, we can refer to euphemisms assigned to the body. Some symbols may be personal, differing from one person to the next, and others may be cultural, differing from one society to the next. Additionally, some symbols may cross societal boundaries, keeping approximately the same meaning at all times. Below is a list of typically American euphemisms. Feel free to add to it, or change it, in order to meet your own symbolic system.

Euphemisms Pertaining to the Body

- Shouldering the burden, The soft shoulder, The cold shoulder
- Holding on, Letting go (hands or digestion), Washing my hands of it, Eating out of the palm of my hand, I can't handle it
- Can't lift a finger to help, Pointing a finger at someone, Giving someone the finger, I've got him (her) under my thumb, Knuckling under, Wrapped around my little finger
- Limp wrists

- Elbow grease, Elbow room
- Spineless, The stab in the back, A pat on the back, Bending over backwards, It's a back breaker, Standing tall, Standing up for yourself, Monkey on your back
- Beating your head against a wall, Hold your head high
- Pain in the neck
- Muscling your way in
- Standing on your own two feet, Putting your best foot forward, Stepping on someone's toes, Getting your feet wet, Fleet of foot, Getting a foot in the door, Dragging your heels, Clay feet, Stuck in the mud, Turning inward or outward (can relate to ankles)
- Kick him where it hurts (can effect knees or genitals)
- Weak in the knees, Knee-jerk reaction
- Jab in the ribs, Thorn in the side
- Two faced, How we face the world (skin), A slap in the face
- Worry wart, (a belief in one's own ugliness)
- Stiff upper lip, Slack jawed, Sink your teeth into something, Tongue in cheek, Bite your tongue, Grit your teeth, Let me chew on that
- Sticking one's nose into others' business, Nose to the grindstone
- A real eyesore, Too angry to see straight, Seeing red, Keep your eyes peeled, I don't want to see that, I don't want to be seen, Looking down on others
- One ear to the ground, Still wet behind the ears
- Makes my skin crawl, Getting under my skin, Jumping out of your skin
- Eat your heart out, Heart ache, broken heart, Wearing your heart on your sleeve, That's a killer
- Head up your butt, All crapped out, Needing to let go of crap, Scared shitless, A pain in the butt, Ants in my pants (nerves)
- It takes my breath away
- I've swallowed enough of that, Can't stomach something, Let me digest that, A gut feeling, A real gut wrencher, All tied up in knots, Butterflies in my stomach, Gnawing away at you, Got a belly full
- Red, Inflamed, Swollen, Boiling over, Makes my blood boil, Reaching the boiling point, (anything with "itis" could be anger)

ANY thought that is continually repeated may sink into the body. It can be the result of past memory, personal symbology or both. The consequence is the same-tension in the related body part. You can take one of your own specific physical patterns of dis-ease and consider how it is related to the function of your body. Consider the physiological AND symbolic applications, and see if there is a euphemism that might apply. See if there is a limiting thought associated with the dis-ease, and explore the history of both the dis-ease and the limiting thought. These steps alone take you further on the road to healing-physically, mentally, and emotionally.

For a complete study of the body, its memory attributes and symbolic applications, please see a partial list of references at the end of this text. The examples contained herein are meant to get you started. Discover your own symbology and work with it!

The Benefits Of Dis-Ease

Another valuable tool in healing the body, as with any other part of the environment, is the ability to see the results of any dis-ease. What am I "getting" from this illness? This is called a secondary gain. For example, isn't it amazing how we can almost completely cure a cold immediately after calling in sick to work? Perhaps the cold served its purpose and allowed us to gain a much-needed rest. When we give ourselves permission to rest, we no longer need the cold. A wonderful text concerning the mental and emotional components of illness is *Getting Well Again* by O. Carl Simonton, MD., Stephanie Matthews-Simonton and James L. Creighton. Although the book deals mainly with cancer, its concepts may be applied to a variety of diseases.

Many times all we need do is give ourselves PERMISSION to have and meet certain needs and wants, rather than being forced to meet those needs. If we merely *want* something such as a day-off, rest and relaxation, emotional support, nourishment and so on, but think we don't *need* it, we may open ourselves up to feelings of unworthiness and guilt. The result-we get dis-eased and force ourselves to meet those needs. This actually serves us because once we "have to" do something, we let ourselves off the hook for merely "wanting" to do it.

The key to wellness is getting our wants and needs met in healthy ways. As a preventative measure, we can instill within ourselves the habit of being aware of, and meeting, our needs BEFORE we get sick.

Changing The Past

Once we discover anything on a thought level either causing or contributing to a pattern of dis-ease, we can proceed with the healing process, preventing further dis-ease. We can release the tension, memory and associated symbolism, and facilitate the healing.

In his book, *Urban Shaman*, Serge King suggests physically replaying the incident immediately following any trauma. For example, referring to the bicycle story presented earlier, I would go through all the actions of getting into an accident without actually hitting anything, and without actually hurting my ankle. I would address the limiting emotional and physical memories, changing them to positive ones.

Barring a physical re-enactment of the original incident, I could do the same thing mentally. Imagining the incident, and replaying it with a positive outcome, I can change the imprint of the experience on my Lower Self without physically re-enacting the incident. *(An exercise, "Gray Screen/White Screen" is presented later in the text when healing specific memories.)*

I could also vow to get boots or high top sneakers, assuring the safety of my ankles. Dealing with the emotional cluster, I could work through my anger toward (and from) authority figures. Making sure I don't have to work too much harder in order to enjoy myself, I could cut expenses, save money, and so on. Working through ANY of these anxiety producing emotional clusters has a positive healing effect on other aspects within that cluster.

In my bicycle story, I got another bike thirty years later and had some additional experiences at that time. Questions I would ask myself are: "Are there any similarities between the two incidents?

What was going on in my life at both times? Is there a common denominator, mentally and/or emotionally, between the two incidents? Was I faced with a certain problem or set of circumstances at both times in my life? Does that part of my body symbolize any limiting thoughts I may have been holding onto in the past or present?"

By answering any or all of these questions, we can see what the limiting thought, emotion or experience was, and explore ways of augmenting the healing process. Through changing the thoughts along with the emotional response, we change the memory relating to the emotional cluster–mentally, emotionally and physically.

Systematic Desensitization:
Relaxing Into the Comfort Zone

First I wish to address any past, painful memories I might have. I could replay the initial bicycle incident, yet race through or delete any hurtful parts in order to change the mental, emotional and physical aspects of that memory. In this way I help to release the limiting memory. I CAN change my memories if I wish to. After all, it's MY memory, and I can do with it whatever I wish.

After releasing the past tension, I can now address the present and future. One behavior modification exercise that could help this process is called Systematic Desensitization. This entails focusing on a goal and mentally playing out the scenario, one step at a time, relaxing with each step in the process. I would first think about getting a bike, and relax. Then I would think about and see myself getting a bike, then think about, get, and ride the bike, and relax. I would continue the process until I can successfully get everything I want and need, and stay relaxed. It is important get to a point of relaxation with each step of the process before continuing on to the next.

Within this process, I would first release any past tension, and create a fulfilling, relaxed memory. I would then focus on the present and future, opening up avenues of fulfillment there as well.

Pairing A Positive Feeling With A Negative Feeling: Defusing The Charge

A variation on this theme, calling for excitation rather than relaxation, can be taken from Neuro-Linguistic Programming (NLP). We can "anchor" a positive experience next to the original incident. Alternately, by recalling the limiting experience along with a positive experience (even if it is something totally unrelated), can defuse an emotional charge. For example, I love to fly fish, and the successes therein are tangible and somewhat ecstatic. I can recall the bicycle incident with a positive outcome, then the fly fishing successes (with all the feelings, sounds and pictures), then the bicycle, the fishing, the bicycle, and so on until I have paired bicycle riding with feelings of success. The positive feelings are now greater than the negative feelings, allowing for a healthy environment--healing the ankle and getting a bike.

Flooding is another behavior modification technique. This involves replaying the incident over and over again mentally and physically until basically, I am too damn tired to get tense and fearful. I can rent a dirt bike (fully insured of course), put on shoulder and knee pads, gloves and helmet, and ride through extremely rough terrain, then traffic. This would change my memory of biking by simply encouraging the fears and going through the tension, but without the limiting consequences. I can ride a regular bike and purposely crash, knowing that with ten layers of protective gear I wouldn't get hut. I would then be free to get a bike of my own, heal my ankle at an accelerated rate, and reduce the likelihood of future injury.

The techniques presented above have one thing in common: experiencing something new, mentally, emotionally and physically, in order to create a new, more positive memory.

Death As Healing

If faced with a terminal illness, the same concept applies. What do the symptoms represent on a symbolic level? What needs are being fulfilled? What are we learning from the dis-ease? Answering these questions, we leap ahead in the healing process. This is not to say that we will always heal ourselves physically. Sometimes the illness, even death, is the healing itself. What we can learn about ourselves and our world through illness, or even death, is astounding.

One Client, Beth, had cancer for some time. She had been seeing doctors for her condition, receiving both radiation and chemotherapy. We explored some of the mental and emotional stressors behind the illness, and came up with what Beth thought was contributing to the cancer. She had been living with her husband for many years, but had grown sad and lonely within that relationship. Being raised to love and honor "till death do we part", she would not give herself permission to leave the marriage. She had wanted to beak away and explore things in her life that would have made her happier, but the anger and guilt she felt was enormous and kept her at home for a long time.

During our work together, her cancer went into remission and she enjoyed her life more fully. Releasing much of her anger and guilt, at the age of 60 she left her husband, got an apartment, went camping, whitewater rafting, hiking and traveling. She became more social and perhaps the happiest she had been for decades.

A year later the cancer returned "with a vengeance", and she deteriorated rather rapidly. Calling her family and friends to her, even her husband, she expressed her appreciation of them and of life. Beth thanked them for the love and support they had given her throughout her life and especially during the past year. With serenity, peace, and no regrets, she passed on an hour or so before her scheduled birthday party. After her death she showed up in my dreams and those of her daughter to thank us for helping her find happiness, and to remind us to move on with life like she did. Who are we to say that death is NOT a healing?

Another client I had seen while working for Hospice as a grief counselor on the bereavement team had recently "lost" his wife to cancer. Bob was having a hard time dealing with her passing. He was aimlessly looking for a sense of purpose in his own life. We talked. We dialogued. We cleared up some limiting thoughts and feelings. He reached a deeper level of completion with her.

After meeting with him over a period of months, he got to the point of moving on with his life. He cleaned out some of his wife's belongings, took up oil painting again, and decided to find fulfillment and enjoyment.

Three months later, Bob's own cancer, which had been in remission for years, brought him to his death bed. He was ready to heal himself, ready to let go of suffering the pain of separation. He passed on peacefully, fulfilling his needs and wants by "joining" his wife. I believe he could have healed himself physically, but instead, he chose to let go of the pain by giving in to his cancer and passing on. His goals had been to love and support himself, receive love and support from others, and to move on with his life. This is exactly what happened.

Healing the healing process itself.

Healing is a process. As we clear one limiting belief or dis-ease, others may surface. We can then continue the process of self-discovery and healing. Be patient. It's taken a lifetime (or more) to program ourselves. Surely we can give ourselves a little time to break the old patterns.

When we are ready to heal ourselves, we do so. The healing may take an infinite number of forms, but it happens!

- - -

- 11 -

The Manifestation Process: Focus Clearly, Breathe Deeply, Believe Completely

And Hercules, with hands only, did conquer Cerberus, the three headed guardian at the gates of Hell, and bring forth Theseus from the Chair of Forgetfulness.

Of the many treatises I have read concerning inner dialogue and Kahuna, Maxwell Freedom Long's *Self Suggestion* is perhaps the simplest and most specific when relating to creative thought, manifestations and healing. He states that in order to effect change within our environment, both internal and external, we can "...think hard, breathe deep, and believe completely."[30] I like to reword that phrase as, "Focus clearly ("think hard" implies too much work), breathe deeply, and believe completely".

Focus clearly

The first step in the manifestation process is to focus clearly. As we develop a personal symbology, we can interpret our creations within the environment. Then, upon seeing what we have created, we can work with our thoughts and memories, discovering what resistance and limitations we may have when trying to meet specific wants and needs.

Journaling is a good way to start focusing on what it is we wish to accomplish. One of the goals of journaling is to have a free and easy inner dialogue between the Middle and Lower Selves. What do you wish to talk about with yourself? You may even want to start journal work by addressing the subject of journal work, dialoguing with yourself about dialoguing. This makes journaling much more effective, and reinforces any changes you may wish to make.

Generally, you can start by writing about thoughts, events of the day, goals, anything that comes up, and then asking the Lower Self for feedback. Dialogue. Respond to the Lower Self using positive thought with a loving and accepting attitude, keeping those thoughts simple, clear and focused. Shortly within this text, we will explore different examples of this process, but it's great to just get things going for now.

Breathe deeply

Another aspect of manifesting positive change within our lives is learning to breathe deeply. With the use of deep breathing, we allow our energies to be freed up, not only physically, but emotionally as well, getting personally involved with the world, with Spirit, and with the healing process. With the breath, we can center, help focus our thoughts and build our energy.

Believe completely

The last and perhaps most important step in creating a new reality is to believe completely. Focusing clearly, we address ways of reprogramming old beliefs. Breathing deeply, we energize ourselves and our thoughts. Believing completely, we can instantly be in touch with that part of ourselves that already has everything we desire. We can affirm a new, more limitless reality, and let it grow. We then see it, feel it, hear it, experience it, and expand on it to include even more.

As we progress in this text we will look at specific methods of journaling. After focusing clearly we will then explore practical methods of using the breath along with positive belief or affirmations in order to change past patterns and apply unlimited creativity to life. In short, we will discover how to put love and power behind our will.

Calling In The Higher Self -
Assuring objectivity, creativity and Love

To start journaling, find a comfortable, private space, one in which you will not be disturbed, and proceed to take several slow, deep, centering breaths. Call in the Higher Self and feel the energy flowing through you, surrounding you, enveloping you in a high state of Love. This helps to suspend the focus of the Middle Self, allowing the other perspectives and realities to be experienced.

For different people, this takes different forms. We can pray, dance, chant, meditate, sing, use a drum, invoke a Guardian Spirit, or call on God in whatever form we see fit. Simply breathing deeply and focusing our intent is ofttimes all that is necessary. The intention here is to call upon our greatest potential, the objective, loving, shouldless parent, the overseer of the other selves. We can even view the Higher Self as that part of us that is the Greater Authority in our lives and empower the Higher Self accordingly.

We call on the Higher Self in order to assure that neither the Middle Self's logic nor the Lower Self's emotions and memories is the authority in our lives. Each self is present in order to balance the other, but sometimes the Higher Self is needed in mediating any conflicts of interest that may arise. The Higher Self, being creative, open to change, and limitless, is concerned with teaching us to better love ourselves and others throughout life.

One simple method of calling in the Higher Self combines both breath and imagery. While taking a few centering breaths (to the abdomen in order to connect with the Lower Self), see Spirit entering the body by breathing White Light into the top of your head. Then breathe it out your heart or hands toward the paper you'll be working with. Affirm that you are doing the journal work in order to heal the environment and to foster love and cooperation among the various parts of yourself. Focus your intention on accomplishing the Highest Good for yourself and all concerned.

Facing Fears to Re-Program the Past

Reassured that the Higher Self is alert and present to guide us, we can then proceed with journaling. One method entails simply asking the Lower Self to express its fears. By acknowledging our fears, we can then take the power away from them. Having a wider range of choices regarding how we can respond to those fears, we are able to tame the "monster in the closet".

The following exercise is adapted from some of Sandra Ray's work presented in her "Loving Relationships Training". First decide what it is that you want and need in your life. That can be anything: physical objects, new relationships, more positive feelings about yourself and others, healing, and so on. Focus on a situation in you life that you wish to improve. Then start with a statement concerning that situation:

"One of the fears I have about _____ is _____."

For instance, if you wish to work on accepting yourself more, the statement might read, "One of the fears I have about loving myself is _____."

Take a deep breath, say the statement as fast as you can, and then fill in the blank. The statement itself comes from the Middle Self, but the response filling in the blank comes from the Lower Self. By saying the statement fast, you do not give the Middle Self time to THINK of the answer. You allow the Lower Self to express itself.

If, at first, you do not get something to fill in the blank, say it again even faster. Be sure to write down the response, whatever fills the blank. You can then continue with the same statement, flushing out any additional fears...

"Another fear I have about loving myself is _____."
"Another fear I have about loving myself is _____."
"Another fear I have about loving myself is _____."

After flushing out several fears, conclude this portion of the exercise with...

"The greatest fear I have about loving myself is _____."

Some responses may be repeated, filling in the blanks two or more times with the same answer. Or perhaps the greatest fear is a repetition of one of the previous fears. This is merely pointing out that that particular response holds significance. Some of the fears may even take you by surprise. They may not make any sense from the Middle Self's perspective. But remember, you are dealing with the Lower Self here, with its perceptions, memories and conclusions.

This exercise may also be used within a therapeutic relationship between two people. The helper and helpee sit facing one another, looking into each others' eyes. The helpee can take a deep breath and say the statement, "One of the fears I have...", while the helper just observes or writes down the response. After the helpee has finished the statement (filling in the blank), the helper simply says, "Thank you." The process then continues as before until the greatest fear is reached.

The helper does not go into sympathy with the helpee. The helper does not reinforce the helpee's fears. The helper just thanks the helpee for sharing, creates a safe atmosphere, and affirms that the world will not come to an end just because a few fears have been acknowledged. The exercise can then be concluded with a nice, heartfelt hug between helper and helpee.

After writing down several of the fears, as well as the biggest fear, you can group them together. Some of those fears may be similar and reflect the same limiting thought. Grouping them together saves much time when trying to access a specific personal law or core belief. I'd like to, once again, use my bicycle story as an example...

"One of the fears I have about getting a bicycle is that I'm afraid of getting into an accident."

"Another fear I have about getting a bicycle is that I'll never get to work on time, and my boss will be angry at me."

"Another fear I have about getting a bicycle is that I'll have to work hard to get the money."

"Another fear I have about getting a bicycle is that I'll probably ride it a lot and my girlfriend will get mad at me."

"The greatest fear I have about getting a bicycle is that others may not support me on getting one."

We may then group the responses:

Response	Limiting Thought
Accident	It's not safe.
Hard Work	It will take a lot of effort.
Boss is angry with me	Others will not support me
Girlfriend is angry with me	Others will not support me.

After grouping the responses, create an affirmation to aid in reprogramming the old tapes, changing the memory. It is best to keep the affirmation as simple and manageable as possible. If you make it longer than one or two sentences, the Lower Self may lose interest. You may also tap into too many fear responses, making it hard to focus clearly, and to effectively dispute ANY limiting responses. So, for your Lower Self's sake, keep it simple!

The completed affirmation, addressing each group of responses may look something like this...

"I am now manifesting the perfect bicycle, safely and effortlessly. I allow others to support me on this."

When thinking about getting a bicycle, when looking for one, or when considering the consequences of obtaining one, you can lovingly introduce the above affirmation into your mind, and relax.

If you find yourself creating any limiting thoughts, automatically take a deep breath and repeat the affirmation to yourself, countering those limitations or fears.

The previously described affirmation method involves discovering fears and limitations first, followed by a constructed (and hopefully perfect) affirmation. Another method of journaling, the "two column approach" (also adapted from Sondra Ray's work[31]) involves first creating a general affirmation or goal. We then allow the space for responses to surface, and end by creating a more complete affirmation.

Focus on an affirmation or goal that applies directly to a given situation, and then list the responses. These "ifs", "ands" or "buts" that the Lower Self presents may be considered "negative responses". They are not bad. Nor are they crazy. They are merely limiting. We call them "negative" because they *negate* the positive thoughts or affirmations.

Affirmation or Goal	Negative Response
I want to get a bicycle.	But I'm afraid of getting into an accident.
I want to get a bicycle.	What if others get angry at me?
I want to get a bicycle.	But I remember the last bike I got. It cost me a lot of hard work and money.
I want to get a bicycle.	Well, I can't afford one now anyway. I should start saving now.

- - -

Completed Affirmation

"I am now manifesting the perfect bicycle, safely, effortlessly, and at the perfect time. I allow others to support me on this."

This exercise may also be done in pairs. The helper first states the initial desire or goal in the "you" form: "You want to get a bicycle." The helpee then says the first response that comes to mind. The exercise continues until there are no more responses, or until some of the previous responses start being repeated. The two people can then join forces and create an effective affirmation.

Real Dialogue Between The Selves

Another method of journaling, one that I prefer, approaches a more natural dialogue. This entails dividing a piece of paper in half lengthwise. On the left side of the paper the Middle Self or parent, can express itself. On the right side, the Lower Self or child, can speak. First relax and take some centering breaths, asking that the Middle (parent) Self identify more easily with the Higher (shouldless parent) Self. By doing so, you do not "should on yourself". You change the "shoulds" into "coulds", and the "can'ts" into "won'ts" or "coulds", allowing more freedom of thought and emotion.

Middle Self, Parent	Lower Self, Child
Thoughts & Intellect	Feelings & Memories
Goals & Desires	Negative Responses
Positive Thoughts	Ifs, Ands, Buts, Can'ts

If there is agreement between the Middle and Lower Selves, with no limiting thoughts expressed by the Lower Self, then we can rest easy. Unless we are blocking limitations from our conscious mind or we are not ready to clear something, our environment will probably reflect our clear and loving perspective. However, if there are limiting thoughts or emotions, we can continue to dialogue in order to reach a more peaceful conclusion to our session...

I really want a bicycle.

It can be safe to ride that bike. You'll just be more aware, and ride safely.

But I'm afraid of getting into an accident.

But then I might be late to work. I'll also ride alone. My boss and my girlfriend will be angry with me.

You can allow other people to support you on this. This is something we can resolve together.

But I remember the last time I got a bike. It cost me a lot of hard work and money.

It can be easy this time. Be open to having it easy.

Well, I can't afford one now. I should start saving money.

Getting one can be easy, too. Be open to having it easy.

Oh. OK. I'll give it a try.

Thank you. I love you. We'll speak later.

- - -

We can then review the personal process we've put on paper and devise a tangible affirmation, a positive thought on which to focus our attention:

"I am now manifesting the perfect bicycle safely, effortlessly, and at the perfect time. I allow others to support me on this."

Even after attaining agreement and cooperation, during future dialogues we can still stay open to acknowledging any fears, any negative responses that may come up. Resistance can surface at any time. For example, imagine a garden hose, something that carries water from the faucet to the garden.

The faucet, where the water enters the hose, is likened to our initial thought, an affirmation, goal or desire. The hose itself represents the individual process when manifesting what we need or want. The garden reflects our environment, where the fruits of our labor are manifested, the Environmental Consequence. However, sometimes there are one or more kinks in the hose, limiting thoughts or fears, obstacles, painful or limiting memories that may hinder us when manifesting more positive things in our life.

If we don't turn on the water in the first place, if we do not wish to grow a nicer garden, who cares about the kinks in the hose? But once we DO turn on the water, those kinks may prevent the garden from getting the nourishment it needs. The same applies to thoughts and energy. If we sit still and don't put energy into manifesting a better environment, then the fears and limitations are not of any consequence. However, once we DO go toward more love and positive change within our lives, the resistance to manifesting those changes may arise.

Love Brings up anything unlike itself.[32]

We can, of course, merely turn on the water and hope it succeeds in getting through to the other end of the hose. The water will get through the smaller kinks, we'll get past smaller limitations. However, if there are big kinks in the hose, the water will hit them and start backing up. We cannot merely force the Middle Self's will upon the Lower Self and ignore the consequences. The energy backs up. The obstacles become greater and greater. The backed up energy creates a dis-eased environment. The larger kinks in the hose or the bigger mental and emotional limitations require more personal attention. This is where dialogue comes in.

Don't Ask Why!

In creating a safe atmosphere for effective dialogue, it is good to avoid judgments, shoulds and limitations, but it is also wise to avoid the word "why". Asking "why" only puts the child within on the defensive, resulting in either justifications, lies, or a total lack of communication.

Additionally, thinking we know "why" things are the way they are, we may inadvertently give ourselves permission NOT to change. I have often talked with people who say, "Once I find out why I am sad or angry, I can release that feeling and get on with the rest of my life." But that thought is limiting in and of itself. Suppose our emotional charge and fear of change prevent us from finding out "why" we feel a certain way? In that case it is better to first acknowledge any limiting thoughts and release the emotional charge surrounding them. Then we may discover why we've had that emotion. It may not even be important anymore because, once a limiting belief or emotion is released, it no longer effects us. We may no longer care "why" we had it in the first place. We then have the freedom to move on with our lives.

If the "why" is important, don't worry, it will come up later.

We do much better by asking the Lower Self "what" it is creating, what the intended result is, and what the consequences of our actions are. "Why" focuses on the problems. "What" focuses on the solutions. We can find out what the Lower Self hopes to accomplish, what hopes, needs and wants are expected to be fulfilled. We can then explore different methods of achieving those goals, in gentle, loving ways.

This is the beginning of dialogue--being open to honest, caring and loving discussion. Disagreements, different points of view, can be worked out with the willingness to focus on solutions. Of course, there may be other negative responses as time goes on. Additional fears and limiting thoughts may surface at a later time. However, they can be addressed, as long as we are open to dialogue!

Talking with our selves, our environment and others around us can be a normal, everyday affair. Healing can be just a thought away.

- - -

- 12 -

Affirmation Dialogue

...and first there was the word.

Journal work is best done before retiring in the evening (or whenever you go to sleep). It is during this time that the conscious mind, the Middle Self, is naturally getting out of the way and allowing room for the subconscious mind, the Lower Self, to express itself. Journaling is also productive upon awakening, when the Lower Self is still strongly in touch with the Middle Self after sleeping and dreaming.

My preference is for approximately ten minutes of journal work daily, or for twenty minutes two ir three times a week. I encourage you to set up some sort of schedule to allow for this. I like to think that ten minutes of journal time is worth at least an hour or two of thinking. If we acknowledge our subconscious beliefs more often, they will not need to manifest so blatantly in order to gain our attention.

In the last chapter we discussed several methods of journaling. One method entailed the two column approach using an affirmation, and then flushing out negative responses. Another method involved beginning with simple dialogue and ending with an affirmation. By combining the two approaches, we now have what I call "affirmation dialogue".

As with other approaches, we still have the positive thought on one side of the paper and the negative response on the other. But with Affirmation Dialogue, we do not merely focus upon positive thought, but upon positive AFFIRMATIONS. We then allow for on-going discussions and continuous changes in the affirmation as we dialogue.

An Affirmation Is Alive!

An affirmation is not just a statement! It is not a stagnant thing meant to be repeated over and over again. If we do that, the Lower Self merely keeps re-stating its negative responses, its limiting thoughts. An affirmation is a living entity, filled with energy and intent. It evokes responses from both the Lower Self in the form of memories, beliefs and feelings, and from the Higher or Creative Self in the form of manifestations within the environment. The Middle Self then has the task of replying to these responses, changing the affirmation if necessary in order to address newly discovered limitations.

Relating to the "kinks in the hose" analogy again, as we take out one kink in the hose, the water may rush forward to the next kink. We put forth the positive energy (turn on the water), allow for the negative response (the kink in the hose), turn once again to the positive energy (another affirmation taking out that kink), and allow for the next negative response (the next kink in the hose). And so on.

This process is also the same within a therapeutic relationship - the helper role plays the shouldless parent, creating affirmations and positive thoughts, while the helpee responds.

Affirmation	Response
Let's focus on getting a bicycle.	
	But I'm afraid of getting into an accident.
I am **safely** manifesting a bike.	
	What if others get angry with me?
	What if I get a bad bicycle?
I am safely manifesting the **perfect** bike. I **allow** others to **support** me on this.	

Affirmation	Response
	But the last time I got a bike. It cost me a lot of hard work and money.
I am safely and **effortlessly** manifesting the **perfect** bike. And I allow others to support me on this.	
	Well, I can't afford one now. I should start saving money.
I am **now** manifesting the **perfect** bicycle, safely, effortlessly, and **at the perfect time**. I allow others to support me on this.	
	OK. I can do that. I'll give it a go.
Thank you. I love you.	

- - -

At any point in the affirmation dialogue process we may get a POSITIVE response. And that's wonderful. This may come in the form of any number of phrases:

• Okay • I guess so • It seems Okay • I'll give it a go • You win • We'll do it • If you want to •

If we do get a positive response, we can immediately thank the Lower Self and consider our work done...for the moment. There may be additional negative responses in the future. If there are, we can trust that they will arise at the perfect time. We will either see them manifest within the environment, or they will surface during journaling or whenever we process about a given situation.

As you can see, even a simple affirmation can have many related negative responses or emotional clusters. This is part of the magic. While still working on something specific, we can also help release resistance in other areas of our lives. As an example, use the above bicycle process

Affirmation Dialogue

A = A = A = A = ...
Bike = Accident = Anger at authority figures = More work = Hurt = Less money = Separation from friends = ...

The affirmation accepted by the Lower Self was, "I am now manifesting the perfect bicycle, safely, effortlessly, and at the perfect time. I allow others to support me on this." This affirmation relates specifically to getting a bicycle. But if you look at the relative emotional clusters, you can see that the positive thoughts may address other areas as well–relationships with authority figures, means of monetary and emotional support, safety issues, and so on.

In actuality, there can be any number of negative responses (and affirmations that counter them) over a period of time that present themselves in this process. For instance, the Lower Self may agree to get the bike, but feel, "OK. Authority figures aren't angry with me concerning this issue, but they're angry about other things." or "I won't separate from friends over this, but there are other people who I don't want to see." There may be any number of responses that arise. We do not need to go into overwhelm here, though. We need only concern ourselves with the responses that come up presently.

We can even simplify the process a little more. In facilitating this procedure with thousands of people throughout the years, I have discovered that the negative responses usually fall into various categories. Additionally, there are various groupings of possible inclusions into the affirmation that can be used to counter typical limiting beliefs. These inclusions make the affirmation more effective and more complete, helping to prevent the negative responses from manifesting too blatantly.

The Affirmation Dialogue below gives examples of common fear-based responses from the Lower Self, followed by phrases that can counter those specific fears. It is best to read the right-hand column first, and then move on to the left-hand column, the Possible Inclusions. Keep in mind that these are only generalized responses to, and inclusions into, the affirmations. This list, along with your own customized additions, provides a firm foundation for creating and modifying any affirmation about any issue.

Affirmation Dialogue

**Possible Inclusions
Into Affirmations**

**Generalized Responses
(Ifs, Buts, Can'ts)**

- but that will take a lot of time

- now
- at the perfect time

- - - - - - - - - -

- but that's hard
- it will take lots of work
- I'll try hard

- effortlessly
- easily

- - - - - - - - - -

- what if I (others) get hurt
- but I (others) will feel sad
- I (others) will feel threatened

- painlessly
- safely
- and I feel safe with that
- and I allow others to feel safe with that
- I allow others to support me on this

I do not have the power to change another person, or to break someone else's free will, so I do not say, "Others feel safe with this." I can affirm what I have control over, and that is "allowing others to feel safe" and "allowing others to support me." If I have done whatever I can in order to allow others to feel safe, then I can also allow them to feel threatened, knowing that either way, I am still okay. I have done what I could, allowed others to do what they will.

- - - - - - - - - -

- in the perfect form
- in whatever form is for the Highest Good (of myself and all concerned)
- All my changes are for the Highest Good.

- but what if it doesn't turn out like I planned
- It's got to be done a certain way
- but I'll have to change

- - - - - - - - - -

- but I'll have to leave
- but I'll be alone
- she/he/others will leave

- and I attract and accept the perfect support for this
- I attract others who feel safe with this.

Again, because I do not have the power to force others to do my bidding, I do not say "others who support me are attracted to me." I need to phrase things from my perspective and my locus of control: "I attract and accept the support." This is within MY power.

Additionally, "attracting and accepting support" is different from "allowing others to support me". "Attracting others who feel safe" is different from "allowing others to feel safe". When I allow others to support me or feel safe, I assume I am in relation with someone and I am doing my best to create a non-threatening opportunity for that person to support me. However, as happens in some relationships, there may come a time when we surrender to the lack of support from our partner, boss or someone else, and I may look elsewhere for support. This does not mean we have to leave a current relationship or job because, sometimes, just the willingness to look elsewhere heals the current situation.

When we attract rather than allow the support, we have already moved on mentally and emotionally from the current relationship.

There may come a time when we feel the need to "physically" and tangibly move on, but that is on an individual basis. The decision must be made personally. Moving on from "allowing others" to "attracting others" creates powerful change within ourselves, and we WILL get the safety and support we need...in whatever form is for the Highest Good.

- - - - - - - - - -
- but I can't trust that to be true
- I can't see that
- I can't accept that
- I don't know if
- I don't believe it

- I, (your name), acknowledge that...(rest of affirmation)

- - - - - - - - -
- I can't
- I won't
- I don't believe it
- That's not true

- I, __, am able (willing) to __
- I, __, am able and willing to __ more easily (effortlessly) __ all the time
- better all the time

The response, "I won't", carries with it a large emotional charge, reflecting a painful or hurtful memory. In addition to a verbal response, some of the negative responses presented may be emotional and need to be dealt with on that level. Forgiveness affirmations later in this chapter address this issue.

Additionally, within mainstream psychological circles, there is a term, made popular by Leon Festinger, called "Cognitive Dissonance". Referring to one's self concept, this term addresses the idea that if someone compliments us at a level too far above our own level of self-esteem and belief, we will automatically discount it.

Affirmation Dialogue

If an affirmation is blatantly too far beyond what we can truly believe, we may ignore it or even try to prove it wrong.

For example, an affirmation of "I express myself perfectly at all times" is certainly an ideal thought to manifest, but it may not be acceptable to the Lower Self. However, "I am expressing myself MORE perfectly at all times" may be easily accepted and then manifested.

- but I don't deserve it
- I am not worthy

- I, __, deserve __
- I, __, love myself and I can __
- I, __, have the right to __

- but I can't change
- change is difficult
- I can't let go of __ (something from the past)

- and all my changes are for the Highest Good (of myself and all concerned)
- easily and effortlessly
- I, __, release any need I have had to __ in the past
- I, __, release any need I thought I had to __ in the past
- Also see the forgiveness affirmations below.

I do not wish to affirm that I HAVE a need to release something in the present, or that I have a PRESENT need to release something, because this may affirm the presence of the thing I wish to release. For instance, I would not wish to affirm that I need to "release my anger" because this affirms that I have a lot of anger presently to release. I would be better served if I affirm that I am "releasing any anger I THOUGHT I had in the past". Instead of affirming that I am "releasing my need to hold on (to something)", I would better serve myself by affirming that "I am releasing any need I have had (or any need I THOUGHT I had) to hold on (to something) in the past."

Forgiveness

- I remember when I was hurt
- but I remember when he (she), (others) hurt me
- It's hard to forgive others (myself) for __
- I can't (won't) forgive others (myself) for __
- I don't deserve it
- but what if I forgive others (myself) and others don't forgive me?
- Generalized or specific anger response

Following is a list of suggested affirmations for forgiveness. I recommend keeping them handy because of the emotional investment many of us have (or thought we had) in holding on to past hurts.

- I can now safely __
- I safely forgive __ for what I THOUGHT he/she/others did to me
- I safely forgive __ for the pain I THOUGHT he/she/others caused
- I safely forgive myself for the pain I THOUGHT I caused __
- I safely acknowledge the love & support I received in the past
- I safely acknowledge the love & support I gave __ in the past
- I safely forgive myself (others) for thinking I (others) did not do __ in the past
- I am willing and able to forgive __ for __
- I am response-able for my life, and I safely acknowledge that others are response-able for their lives

Affirmation Dialogue

- I make my own decisions, and I safely acknowledge that others make their own decisions
- I safely ALLOW myself to feel my own feelings, and I safely ALLOW others to feel their feelings
- I allow others to feel safe with my (their) needs, wants and feelings
- I allow myself to feel safe with my (others) needs, wants and feelings
- I can safely empower myself and others at all times (better at all times)
- I safely express my needs, wants and feelings (my power) (and I allow others to do the same)

To any of these affirmations we may add:

- and I allow others to feel safe with that
- I allow others to support me on this
- I allow others to gain life and enlightenment from this

Forgiveness can be challenging sometimes because of past emotions or present hurtful situations. We do not wish to affirm that others, or ourselves, have caused pain in the past or present. If I forgive someone for the pain "they caused", I affirm that they caused the pain and I BLAME them for that pain. It is better to forgive them for the pain "I THOUGHT" they caused, or for the pain "I felt". In this way I take response-ability for any part I may have played in that scenario. I take response-ability for MY feelings. I also take response-ability for the pain I remember, and for the pain I may need to let go of. This actually gives me a much better sense of control over my own well-being. I am not at the mercy of others.

Also, by forgiving myself for the pain "I caused", I am affirming my own blame and taking response-ability too far by assuming that I have power over others. To alleviate the tendency to blame myself, I affirm that "I release (or forgive myself for) the pain I THOUGHT I caused."

Additionally, by stating that I or others "caused" something, I create and affirm a painful memory, one that may not be accurate, one that assigns blame for things that may not have taken place. "The pain I THOUGHT I (others) caused" allows for more accurate memories, and allows us to change our perceptions. We get to take response-ability, but without the blame.

I also wish to include the phrase "in the past" in order to avoid affirming the presence of pain in the present. An affirmation, after all, puts energy behind what we choose to manifest now. By forgiving whatever we thought happened in the PAST, we are affirming a pain-free existence NOW.

Affirmation dialogue allows us to "focus clearly" on our thoughts and feelings, on exactly what we wish to manifest, what changes we need to make, and what (if anything) from the past we need to release. It helps us affirm the positive and let go of the negative, turning on the water and taking out the kinks in the hose.

Releasing Anger Peacefully and Constructively

There are many ways to release anger: We can beat up someone, burn down a house, get sick, kick the dog or hurt ourselves We can store it up until we are ready to burst, and then take it out on whomever is available. I do not recommend the above methods. For one thing, they are blameful and harmful. For another, they only affirm that having and expressing strong emotions is harmful. Additionally, we then create another reason to blame.

More constructively, we can scream, beat up a pillow, or take a harmless foam bat and hit someone or something. Yet even these methods may seem too violent for some people. They may also affirm the anger unless we follow them immediately with some loving acts.

One simple technique of which I am particularly fond is called "Burning Karma". It is harmless and relatively quiet. With the use of paper and pencil, we will not hurt ourselves, and the neighbors will not call to see if someone is mortally wounded.

Karma may be referred to as any energy we hold onto that may be harmful to ourselves and/or others. I do not feel that it is this BIG thing we carry with us throughout the millennia, this BIG lesson that we need to learn in order to get off the Buddhist "Wheel of Life". Rather, it is something that prevents us from forgiving ourselves and others, something that gets us stuck in the past. My personal belief is that the only Karma we have this lifetime is to learn to release Karma lovingly and harmlessly. We can let it go and move on.

Burning Karma

Situate yourself in a private, comfortable space. Have several (many) pencils available and at least a dozen or so sheets of paper.

After taking a few deep centering breaths and relaxing, call in the White Light, the Higher Self, and affirm that you do not mean any harm to yourself, to God, or to anyone else. Affirm that you are releasing any emotions in order to heal relationships, not harm them.

Next, focus on whomever you may be angry at, be it someone else, God, or yourself. Taking a pencil to the paper, call that person every name in the book. You may even wish to hold the pencil like a child, gripping it within your closed fist. Huff and puff, and release those emotions on paper.

Get into it! Let it out! Purge yourself of that anger and sadness. Speak your mind, name what's unfair, unjust, and hurtful. Curse, blame, vent! You may find yourself ripping paper, breaking pencils, writing so emotionally that you may not be able to read what you've written. You may find yourself crying. That's OK. Let it out. You'll know when you are finished because you'll feel drained, purged, or empty - maybe even quiet and peaceful.

When complete, either rip up the paper into small pieces and throw them out, or burn the paper, affirming that these limiting feelings are released. Then treat yourself nicely. Love yourself. If you do not release the energy completely, find someone with whom to talk, or burn more Karma at another time. However, for now, IMMEDIATELY go and do something loving, something that makes you feel good. Affirm that those emotions are behind you, and that they will not get in the way of your enjoying life.

There have been times when I've felt the need to Burn Karma several times in one day! Other times, I've only felt the need every month or so. Even if I don't exactly know what I am angry or frustrated about, I can Burn Karma by focusing on the frustration of not knowing what I'm frustrated about. At least it's a place to start. The true cause(s) of that anger become apparent as I move along within my individual process. Keep in mind that there is usually hurt and/or fear behind any angry response, for I would not feel angry unless I was hurt and afraid of being hurt again.

The Child's "Mad Pad"

As a therapist or parent, we can call Burning Karma a "Mad Pad" session. Several years ago we bought one of our children a "Mad Pad". Instead of going to her room and destroying the place, she used a special (BIG) pad and a set of special (BIG) crayons. We encouraged her to scribble or draw anything she wanted, letting out her anger on paper. The only rules we had concerning these implements of destruction were that she could use only those particular crayons with that particular pad, and that she had to throw out any drawings she made when finished.

Feeling our feelings, we can get to the thoughts behind them. Changing the thoughts, we can change the feelings and manifest a better world for ourselves and others.

Additional tools for letting go of emotional charges will be discussed later in this text when we deal more specifically with forgiveness and personal power. For now, though, we can use anger release to support us in focusing clearly on what we truly wish to accomplish.

Journaling is an affirmation in and of itself. It affirms that we have some control over our lives. Releasing our limitations safely and lovingly, we affirm that we are learning to love and accept ourselves and others–we are constantly growing.

In one respect, all we are really doing here is changing our personal symbolism. For many people, being aware of limitations symbolizes being stuck. But through journaling and release we change that symbolism to something positive. Awareness is a gift to cherish and use for healing. Being aware of our ability to release negative responses in constructive ways, we affirm our willingness to experience and release resistance. I'm reminded of a quote of Gerald Jampolsky in his book *Love Is Letting Go Of Fear*, "when in doubt, fear forward."

We have turned on the water in the hose. We have introduced positive thought. Now let's put feeling behind those thoughts.

- - -

- 13 -

Personal Power & Forgiveness

Unleashing the forces within me, they traveled far and wide. The power, the feelings, the passion, the storm in all directions. I cannot control those forces, but perhaps I can direct them.

Power is the ability to effect change within the environment. We are constantly in a state of expressing our power, for stifling it would mean stagnation and dis-ease.

Working with thoughts and emotions is fine. Releasing the stress is great. Doing the internal work IS productive. But sooner or later it is time to interact with the environment in more direct ways. This is where our personal power will be put to the test: Can I outwardly create that which I inwardly desire?

Life is about change and power, influencing the world around us. It is necessary to exercise and express our power but, rather than letting that power run rampant, we can direct it in a positive manner. Rather than getting into power struggles within relationships, we can explore ways of affirming our power AND the power of others.

Think of a little child who wants something. If he demands it, reaches for it, and takes it away from someone else, then he is abusing his power. If he asks for it, reaches for it, and gets it appropriately, then he is using his power. There is a constant need to acknowledge personal power and to express it: But does that mean "using" the power or "abusing" it? To a child there is not much of a difference because his primary objective is to meet his needs and wants.

As parents, we teach the child to use personal power without the intent of hurting others. We can nurture that child when he uses his personal power appropriately, and discourage him when he misuses it. We teach him about win-win situations, compromise, and respect for others. As adults, we are still learning the difference between use and abuse of power, knowing when to use it and when not to use it, when to push for something and when to back off. Only now we must parent ourselves.

If we constantly need to prove our personal power, we may try to overpower others, inviting power struggles and conflict. This reflects the Warrior stance, ever vigilant to the possible loss of power. Yet, like the school bully, we become threatened when someone else comes along who is meaner and tougher than we are. A power struggle ensues.

A problem also arises if we hold back our personal power. We may have a thought, "our personal power threatens other people." If that is the case, we may not express ourselves when necessary. Holding in our power, we become "powerless". But sooner or later, anger and resentment build. We get ready to burst. Becoming either passive-aggressive or aggressive, we lash out at people, only proving to ourselves, once again, that "our personal power threatens others." Additional power struggles may ensue.

The way out of this dilemma is to express our feelings and use our personal power when appropriate...allowing others to feel safe, and encouraging others to use their own personal power. Being an Adventurer, I rejoice in my power and love, as well as in the power and love within others. For within relationships, if both parties feel safe, using rather than abusing power, then cooperation and love are easily attainable.

Personal power can be expressed in a variety of ways: physically, emotionally, mentally and Spiritually. On a physical level, personal power means being in balance, having a powerful, dynamic, effective relationship with all that surrounds us and all that is within us. On a

Spiritual level it means putting our personal power behind our Love, using our power for the Highest Good of ourselves and all concerned. On a mental level it means working with our thoughts and not empowering our fears and limitations. On an emotional level it means acknowledging our feelings and letting them be known to ourselves and to others within relationships. Sure, we are vulnerable whenever we let others know our feelings. But there is always a choice-keep those feelings hidden or let them be known. Keeping them hidden, we feel incomplete. There is always something left undone, unsaid. Energy is spent keeping feelings in check, and personal power is diminished.

Being incomplete only gives power to the incompletion.

By worrying, we give power to our fears and limiting thoughts. The feelings and stresses build, creating a state of dis-ease. This may result in even more incompleteness, more emotional charge, hurt, anger or pain. This, in turn may lead to even more incomplete situations within our lives. Fortunately, there are alternatives!

We are not at the end of the path of enlightenment, so of course we may still have power issues. We may still have conflicts with others around us. We may get upset, perhaps angry, and then need to decide how to use our personal power. Rather than stopping ourselves from expressing our feelings and personal power, we can take off the limitations. We can ALLOW others to feel safe with our expression of self. We cannot MAKE others feel safe with what we do, but we can allow them to feel safe. Conversely, we can also allow others to feel threatened, but that is a choice that THEY make.

Being certain of the power and love we ALL carry within us, we can trust others to get past their fear and be in touch with their own personal power. We can express our personal power and HELP others get in touch with theirs. Communicating assertively makes this possible. Knowing that we are doing whatever is necessary to create harmony within our lives, relationships become honest.

Being in a state of completion, we will not let the past get in the way of expressing ourselves in the present.

If we blame others for the wrongs we think they've done to us, we are saying that someone besides ourselves has control and power over our lives. If we blame others for our hurt feelings, we are saying that they have more control over our lives than we do. Additionally, whenever we blame ourselves for others' hurt feelings, even when we've done everything we could to prevent that hurt, then we also give away our power. Remember, the other person may also have his or her own power issues, too. Blame only serves to keep us in a victim role and provide us with REASONS to continue the power struggle.

Such creative ways to deny our personal power! Without blame and projection, we can express ourselves but still acknowledge the other person's feelings and power.

Working through the maze of feelings is a lifetime endeavor. Learning how to express those feelings is a holy task.

We still have the right to feel anger, pain or sadness, but we give away personal power every time we assign blame. We can reclaim our power by communicating! This does not mean taking power away from others. We cannot MAKE others do our bidding. We can just ask for what we want and then leave others' decisions up to them. "I feel ___, I want ___, I need ___, I am willing (or not willing) to ___," are good places to start.

Whatever the specific manifestation, we need to release any anger healthfully, WITHOUT blaming ourselves or others. The first step in clearing personal power issues is self-talk--affirming the positive, and seeing where any resistance lies. Explore the feelings. Clear the thoughts. It is alright to feel all the feelings, both positive and negative.

If we didn't love ourselves, we wouldn't feel hurt or angry.

We are human, therefore we are emotional beings. Our hurt and anger allows us to acknowledge our love. The love allows us to acknowledge our hurt and anger. We have every right to feel angry if we have been hurt. But, again, we can learn to respond with love and acceptance, blessing the other person as we bless ourselves.

It is necessary to acknowledge our anger if we have it. Unacknowledged anger can lead to a course of self-destruction, whether that be violence, suicide or even a tendency to attract accidents or unwanted events. I have found that most, if not all, car accidents and/or other major accidents are preceded by a period of anger in the "victim's" life. Amazingly enough, by acknowledging and releasing that anger, the person may heal his or her body faster and more completely after such an accident. The person may also prevent a recurrence of such unwanted events within his life.

After acknowledging any limiting emotions such as anger or sadness, release them...constructively! Take a break from the situation, yell, cry, scream, beat up a pillow, let the thoughts and feelings out on paper. But do it without harming yourself or others, without giving yourself more reasons to be angry, hurt and blameful. If need be, get help and support from a friend, a parent, a child, a dog, a therapist, anyone you can lean on who would listen and empathize.

Avoiding blame

We can experience the urge to blame others or ourselves, but again we can release that urge without acting on it. If we have had a problem with someone, we CAN release the anger constructively.

First, take some centering breaths. Surround yourself with the Light and affirm that you are releasing this energy for healing. Then write a series of blame letters. The first one is written to someone with whom you have been angry. Blame that person for everything that went wrong in your life, in your relationship with that person, in that person's relationship with others, and so on. While you're at it, what the heck, blame him or her for the deteriorating ozone layer as well. When finished, either burn the letter, rip it into tiny pieces, or throw it out. Do NOT give it to the other person.

Write the second letter to yourself. Accept total responsibility for anything wrong. Blame yourself for anything and everything. Then dispose of that letter, too.

After tapping off the high emotional charge related to blaming someone else and/or yourself, you are now ready for the third and final letter--a loving, more objective one. You can send this letter, use it as a "practice" letter, or talk with the person involved. By expressing your anger and hurt lovingly, you are at least giving him or her a CHANCE to acknowledge your feelings. The other person can then acknowledge his or her part in the situation without getting defensive.

We can own up to our own emotions. The sadness and/or anger is ours! Our emotions are ours! How we respond to others is how WE respond! How we respond to our own emotions is how WE respond! We are the ones who CHOOSE to feel a certain feeling and respond in a particular way. No one has the power to make us feel or act in a certain manner unless we give it to him. We are ALL just doing our best this lifetime to deal with our conflicting needs and wants.

Be motivated to forgive!

Once we have released the anger, or at least some of it, we are then ready for forgiveness. As a motivation to forgive someone, know that we are empowered when we take response-ability for our own feelings. Forgiving others, we feel complete with a given situation, affirm our own choices, and move on. As a last resort, I may sometimes joke with my clients and students, "If you can't do anything worse to your 'enemies', forgive them, it leaves them feeling real bad."

Another means of acquiring the motivation to forgive is to see the offending person, in your own mind, as a frightened little child: it's easier to forgive a frightened child than an angry adult. Besides, we then get to feel good about ourselves because WE play the role of the loving, accepting person.

Once we have ranted and raved, released some of the high emotional charge, perhaps written a series of blame letters, we can then continue the forgiveness process. We can use self-talk and journaling to help us focus more clearly on exactly what it is that we are sad or angry about. Focusing on the Highest thought possible relating to the disturbing situation, we can apply that thought directly to our lives. An example of this may be, "I safely acknowledge response-ability for my choices, I acknowledge that others are response-able for their choices."

Hold that affirmation in mind as you participate in the following exercise.

This meditation is a wonderful tool for attaining a state of forgiveness and for energizing ourselves and others. Although it can be done anytime, it is best done before or on the way to sleep. When drifting off to sleep, we are not only better able to connect with our own Lower Self, the subconscious mind, but with subconscious mind of others as well.

During the meditation, we will focus on two distinct areas of the body. The first is the top of the head, called the Crown Center, the part of the body that symbolizes Spiritual energy and the Higher Self. The second part of the body is the Solar Plexus or diaphragm area. This is the Power Center which contains our breathing apparatus. Although the abdomen is the seat of the Lower Self, the subconscious, where we direct the breath and build up our power, it is the Solar Plexus that dictates how, when and where we express that power. Additionally, the Solar Plexus is often one of the first areas of the body to get tense due to emotional stressors. So let's free it up.

The White Heart Meditation[33]

Relax and take some centering breaths. Call in the Light and affirm your willingness to heal a specific situation. Affirm your willingness to communicate with love rather than with anger and/or sadness.

Think of someone with whom you are angry, someone toward whom you may be holding a grudge, or someone who may be holding a grudge against you. It may be someone with whom you are having a hard time communicating. Hold a picture of that person in your mind.

Take a few slow, deep breaths, and envision the White Light entering the top of your head, traveling down to the Solar Plexus. On the outbreath, imagine that Light leaving your Solar Plexus. With every breath, you are now breathing Love and Light through your Crown to your Solar Plexus. You are breathing it out your Solar Plexus...

Send a little white heart out along a cord from your Solar Plexus, and have it enter the other person's Solar Plexus. Keep channeling the Light into your head, through you, to the other person. This way you are giving that person more than just your own energy. You are giving him a Higher energy. Since you are channeling him the energy, you cannot be drained. You are empowering him AND yourself...

Along that cord, communicate anything you've wanted to, anything that is incomplete or that may have been said before but not listened to. Express it now, but with Love rather than with anger. You can even let him know you are or have been angry with him. You can tell him you are angry in a loving way, claiming your anger as your own and not projecting blame on him nor anyone else.

You are communicating from your Lower Self to his. See him as a frightened little child. It was his fear that earlier caused him not to listen. It was his fear that made him react with anger and made him wish to inappropriately take control of the situation. Think of how much power he had given away or was robbed of in order to make him want to take power away from others. Forgive that little child.

It is always easier to love and forgive a frightened little child than it is to forgive an angry, controlling adult.

Send a lot of love to that child. Mentally and emotionally give that child a hug. Let that child hear and accept what you have to say. Review your relationship and see if there is anything else which needs to be said. Send all communications with love. If you can send someone more love and Light than he can send you anger, then you have the situation licked. At least you have done all you could to get back to a harmonious relationship.

Now send him the affirmation that you created earlier. Communicate it in the "I" form. For example, "I now accept response-ability for my feelings, and I allow others to take response-ability for theirs." Send the positive thought along with the appropriate feelings and images. Do it like you mean it!

When complete, while still channeling the Light, see the heart within his Solar Plexus starting to grow. It continues to grow until it totally surrounds him. Still channeling the Light, make the heart brighter and brighter, until there is nothing left but a big, bright heart.

Know that he DID hear what you said. Whether he listens or not is his choice. Know that he DID feel the Love you shared. Whether he acknowledges that feeling or not is his choice, not yours! You have done what you could, the rest is up to him.

Now slowly come out of the meditation (or drift off to sleep if you haven't already), feeling the love, the joy, and the new level of completion you have just given yourself.

- - -

This meditation is good for completing the past. It does not, however, take the place of directly speaking with, or writing to, the other person. But it helps. Additionally, be aware of any need of yours to have the other person understand and/or accept your point of view, and be willing to release control of his response. If another person wishes to control you, or wishes not to end a certain situation with you, he may have no motivation for understanding or accepting you. This is true especially if it is known that his understanding will help you to leave the situation. If this is the case, then you may need to be complete with that person whether or not he is complete with you.

We can maintain our personal power and integrity even if those around us do not maintain theirs.

Since this exercise is used for OUR deeper level of completion, we can use it if we cannot physically get in touch with a person from the past. In conjunction with this idea of completing the past, I recommend making a list of ALL unfinished communications. Don't worry if that list is rather lengthy - it's taken a lifetime to grow to its present length. Pick at least one person per week from that list and complete the communication. If necessary, experiment with the series of blame letters first. Then write the person at his or her LAST KNOWN ADDRESS.[33]

The letter you send is for healing and completion, NOT to renew the relationship, NOT for the purpose of being forgiven or for getting ANY response whatsoever. It is for completion. The worst thing that could happen is that the other person may think you're crazy, but that's okay. Since you are doing this without the investment in a certain response, what do you really care what the other person thinks of you anyway?

I stress to write the person at their last known address because many people have moved by the time you've gotten around to these letters. If this is the case, write the letter without a return address, and just send it out to the universe. You can also use the White Heart Meditation to facilitate the completion. You can do whatever it takes in order to complete the past and move on to the present and future.

One technique, taken from *The Sorcerer's Crossing*[34] involves what Sorceress Clara Grau calls recapitulation. This involves recalling all the feelings and thoughts associated with a specific situation or person. While doing so, look to the left and breathe in deeply, breathing in any power you may have left behind in that specific situation. Then look to the right and breathe out completely, bringing the power back to the present and future. Continue doing this until you are purged of any limiting thoughts and feelings from the past.

To aid in this process, a therapist can be of great help. An additional useful technique is Eye Movement Desensitization And Reprocessing (EMDR).[35] EMDR calls for eye movements from side to side while desensitizing and reprocessing past limiting thoughts and feelings. I encourage you to look into it, experience it from a trained professional, and learn to use it yourself.

Releasing hindrances to our love and power is of utmost importance when trying to manifest a healthy environment.

The White Heart Meditation also helps to open up new doors to the future. If you anticipate having a hard time communicating with a person tomorrow, do this exercise tonight on your way to sleep. This opens up the psychic communication channels between the two of you and helps you to feel calmer and more centered when speaking with that person.

After doing this exercise several times, the pictures, feelings and thoughts associated with it become imprinted in memory. They are then available at any time. In an emotionally charged situation, draw in the Light on the inbreath, and on the outbreath channel it to the other person, surrounding him with it. You will instantaneously bring back the associated images, thoughts and feelings of Love, Light and PERSONAL POWER. The white heart can be used spontaneously, with pre-meditation, during Shamanic Journeying or anytime. When feeling the need to bond with someone or something on a Higher level, sit, breathe, and channel the Love and Light.

When wishing to identify with or bless the Spirit of someone or something (an object, goal, animal, plant or anything), start with the White Heart. If you wish to do a healing on or for someone, start with the White Heart. When using the Shamanic art of merging or shapechanging, start with the White Heart. (Some Shamanic practitioners prefer to connect with objects through the navel.) Experiment with it. Use it. Apply it whenever and wherever appropriate.

Please note that this meditation is potentially very powerful. I encourage you to focus your intent clearly upon the healing aspect of communications. Do not abuse this exercise by focusing your intent on overpowering another person. If you try to overpower someone in this way, you will attract anger and power struggles in return, if not with that person or situation, then with another. What ye sow, so shall ye reap. So let us sow love and empowerment. It WILL be returned.

Now that we've gained some tools for completing the past and preparing for the future, we can spend more time in the present. We do not need to give away our power to old, unfinished communications, to future worries, or to other people. We can focus our intent upon love, healing, and completion.

We can empower our daily lives.

- - -

- 14 -

Hear It, See It, Feel It, Heal It!

Hera, being a vengeful Goddess, did cast her husband's son out of the Heavens to be killed amongst the mortals. And then the birth of something new, something of wonder, power, and beauty was born.

We've already explored how present feelings tap into past memory, triggering additional feelings based on that memory. We've also explored ways of releasing any emotional charge related to that memory. We've talked about changing some of the limiting beliefs that may have been "caused" by that memory. It is now time to take this one step further--to heal our memories.

Experience becomes memory the INSTANT we experience it. So let's create a new experience and change the memory itself.

Memory is not always reliable!

No matter how many ways we look at it, memory is not always factual. Memory comes from the mind, from the past, from what WE remember. And it can be far different from the actual events.

Consider the following example.

At about the age of six or seven, my brother and I were fighting in the back seat of our mom's car. We were driving up a hill. There were cars parked on both sides of the street. Because of the steepness of the hill, it was hard to see what was up ahead. So when my mother came upon a stop sign, it was with very short notice. Screeching to a halt, she avoided going through the intersection and having an accident. BUT, my brother and I went flying. His head hit my face, breaking my nose.

I remember that incident in detail. Everything about it is crystal clear. However, talking with my mom thirty years after the "fact", I discovered that my memory was not based on reality, but on the story concocted for the insurance company.

The cars, the hill, the intersection, the stop sign...they were all lies! The "true" story, surfacing after many years, was very simple. My brother and I were fighting in the back of the car. He hit my nose and broke it. End of story. So much for memories.

One thing that we have all probably experienced is "selective listening". Someone is talking with us, yet only half of what is said sinks in. We only hear a portion of what is expressed. We may also have been emotionally "triggered" by one thing that was said and, while reacting emotionally to that one thing, we become unable to listen to anything that is said afterward. We may only experience a part of any total event.

Having only experienced and/or remembered a part of the total situation, we may then get into an area called "selective memory". We are more likely to remember those things from the past that had an emotional charge connected to them. The greater the emotional charge, the greater the chance we will remember a particular incident (with the exception of repressed memories due to too much trauma, resulting in overload, and memory shut down). The reverse is true as well. If the relative emotional charge is not that great, there is a likelihood we will not remember some or all of the entire event.

Referring to my broken nose memory, perhaps there was more of an emotional charge attached to the false memory than to the true memory. Thus, I chose to carry the false memory with me throughout the years. As a further example, many children may feel wronged by their parents and may grow up remembering those wrongs. They may have a tendency to forget the "rights". This is fairly natural, in that the wrongs are usually emphasized with greater emotional charge. We may all, at times, selectively listen to and remember only the highly charged emotions, ignoring the more "gentle" ones.

I don't encourage doubting every memory, but there are some things that are important to question, such as those prominent experiences that contribute to limitations in the present. As adults, years after an event, we may need to consciously try to remember the positive side of an experience, not only the negative side. We may also wish to attach a greater emotional charge to the love, rather than to the fear, anger and pain that we experience now or remember from the past. In the case of repressed traumatic memories, we may need to remember (or think we remember) the negative aspects of an experience, and then change them to positive aspects.

Being in control of the past, the past will not control us.

Changing The Past

We can balance ANY negative memory with a positive one. This can be done even if we need to IMAGINE the positive experiences. We have a right to empower our positive memories since they can help us to feel better NOW!

Gray Screen - White Screen

For this exercise, let's use my bicycle story as an example. The affirmation I came up with states, "I am now manifesting the perfect bicycle, safely, effortlessly, and at the perfect time. I allow others to support me on this." I repeat this affirmation to myself as I close my eyes and relax, taking some deep, centering breaths.

I imagine myself in a movie theater. I am sitting in one of the seats, and before me is a huge Gray movie screen. I take a centering breath and, on the outbreath, repeat the affirmation to myself. I take another deep breath and hold it in. I ask myself to remember an incident from the past that totally contradicts the affirmation–in this case an event in which I didn't feel safe getting a bike and didn't get the support I needed. When I remember that negative experience, I let out the breath. (This is actually a set up. I WILL remember a negative experience if I need to hold the breath until I do remember it.) I let the negative experience play out on the movie screen in front of me...

I get into an accident and hurt myself. My father is angry. He's yelling at me. I am too young to be response-able. What do I know? He didn't support me on getting that bike in the first place, and now I have to work hard to pay off the damage to my bike and the car. He's yelling at me, belittling me. I feel rotten. While remembering this, my blood pressure may rise, my muscles become tense, and my breath becomes short and shallow. I get hot and flustered as I alternate between wanting to yell back and wanting to just shrivel up into a little ball, disappearing for eternity...

When finished replaying the limiting memories, feeling I can't stand it anymore, I "Blow Away" the movie screen. I make a black "X" over the screen. I blow it up with dynamite, cut it to shreds with a sword, or huff and puff and blow it away.

Taking a few deep centering breaths, I see a bright White movie screen before me. On that screen, I can do several things.

(1) I can replay the same general theme of the event, yet change the setting in which it takes place, the context. Perhaps I can see my Dad in his underwear, I can see a couple of green dwarfs behind him making faces, his voice comes out as a little squeak, the car was a worthless piece of garbage even before I hit it, and so on.

(2) I can replay that incident, first forward, then backward, then forward and backward again until I feel in control of the memory.

(3) I can replay the whole incident as it was and just change the ending in a positive way, or

(4) This is the one I recommend: I can replay the incident in a totally positive manner, in such a way that both my father's and my

needs are met. I get into the accident, but my father comes to me with love. My body begins to heal itself instantly, while my Dad affirms that I've just grown up a bit more. I'll be more careful and responseable in the future, and he'll help me with that, gently and lovingly. We'll work together to get the bike and the car fixed.

Realizing my willingness to learn and grow from the experience, he gives me token work to do so that he can feel he has a part in teaching me a valuable lesson. My fixed bicycle is great. My relationship with my Dad is freer and closer. My body heals. The world is wonderful.

While remembering the experience, my breath is deep and relaxed. My blood pressure is normal. I can sit tall and straight and proud. The love I have for myself and my Dad fills me until I'm ready to burst.

I focus on the White Screen. It comes closer and closer, growing bigger and brighter. The Light shines through me and, as the screen washes over me, the positive feelings engulf me. I feel tremendous relief as a tingling sensation starts at my face and spreads over and throughout my body--my head, neck, shoulders and so on. I become totally surrounded by, and filled with, the Light.

- - -

After doing this exercise, I can now remember the negative event, but I have linked it with a positive experience. The negative charge is now balanced by the positive. In Neuro-Linguistic Programming (NLP) language[36], I have just "collapsed a negative anchor" and instituted a positive one, desensitizing myself to the painful experience. I am now less likely to avoid this memory. Additionally, I am less likely to avoid situations in the present that could possibly remind me of that past incident. I am less likely to be late to work, get into an accident or hurt that same foot. I will not create other expenses in order to avoid fixing the bike I now have or to avoid getting a new one. I will not so easily get angry with authority figures or have authority figures angry with me, and so on. The benefits are endless.

Because of a neutral, or even positive, emotional charge, I am freer to respond to the present without the weight of the past dragging me down.

True, I may have just "made up" this positive experience. But since my memory isn't reliable in the first place, why not reconstruct my memory in order to produce a more positive feeling about myself and others? At the very least, I am better able to remember any positive feelings from that situation, and I am better able to see my relationship with my father in a more positive light. I have also just opened the door to other positive experiences in my life.

- - -

Continuing The Healing;
Focus Clearly, Breathe Deeply, & Believe Completely

This exercise is a tool for helping release limitations from the past. It is, however, not a cure-all. Some experiences may be too traumatic to completely heal in this way. If there comes a time when we wish to receive help in releasing these hindering emotions, we may want to see a therapist or counselor. We may wish to seek out a particular type of therapy, focusing on memory desensitization and/or emotional release. Rebirthing, Reichian Breath Therapy, Neuro-Linguistic Programming, Hypnotherapy, Primal Scream, Rage Therapy, Rolfing, Gestalt, Psychodrama, Eye Movement Desensitization and Reprocessing, and Thought Field Therapy are but a few of the techniques available. Just talking with someone or joining a support group may help.

Shamanic Techniques;
Tangibility, Repetition & The Voice of Authority

Some Shamanic techniques are also useful here. We can contact a Shamanic practitioner and avail ourselves of one or more healing ceremonies. (1) Relative to letting go of the past, we can get a "Spirit Extraction". In some cultures, dis-ease is seen as a living entity, a spirit or object that does not belong within the environment and/or the body. The extraction consists of the Shaman drawing or sucking out the illness, then replacing it with something positive and healthy.

(2) "Psychopomp" work, dealing with those spirits who have passed on, may be done. If a person has passed on yet becomes "Earth-Bound" for one reason or another, the Shaman can help him or her complete the journey to the Spiritual realms. Help is also given to the "living" person when releasing the spirit of a loved one. Grief work is always useful, if only to let go of a part of us that is already dying, a part we no longer need. We can then rely on ourselves more, rather than on the deceased.

(3) A "Power Object Retrieval" can be used to implant the experience and memory of an object that can be used mentally, emotionally and physically to gain strength, power and love. The Giving of Gifts exercise is similar to this. Yet, if it is done by a Shamanic practitioner it may be more tangible, and therefore more useful to the Lower Self.

(4) A "Power Animal Retrieval" can be used, bringing back a power animal that may have left us in the past because of ignorance, trauma or other causes. With the return of a power animal, we can identify with that animal's characteristics and have more resources available to us in any situation.

(5) We can also have a "Soul Retrieval" performed for us. Psychologically, when we experience physical and/or emotional trauma, we may "bury" or "disown" a part of ourselves. Therapy consists of desensitizing ourselves to the original trauma, owning the buried part, and integrating it into our lives once again. From a Shamanic perspective, though, that part actually deserts us. We are left without the capacity to deal with the original situation or with any

similar events occurring afterward. The Shaman travels to the spirit realm, counseling and convincing that lost part of us to return. With that soul part's return would come additional memories as well as the strength and clarity to deal with those memories.

From a Shamanic standpoint, everything is alive and has a spirit. The power object, the power animal, the spirit to be extracted, the lost soul part being returned and thoughts themselves, are all REAL. I believe them to be real, but I can not say that you "should". It doesn't make a difference to the Lower Self whether they are real, metaphorical, or symbolic. With tangibility, repetition, and authority, healing works. More important than what we do for healing is how we use it.

Creating The Future:
Manifestation and Healing Become Everyday Events

Think of the three selves as being different intensities of light. The Middle Self, with its intelligence and involvement in everyday reality, is a normal flashlight. Its intensity is average, but it can focus fairly well on a single object (in this case, a goal). The Lower Self, on the other hand, is a floodlight. Its intensity and emotional charge is great, but its focus is scattered. The thoughts and feelings may start from a central location, but they diffuse outward in many directions.

Working with affirmations, we combine the Focus of the Middle Self (through journaling and awareness), with the Intensity of the Lower Self (through repetition and tangibility), and project our thoughts and feelings with accuracy AND intensity. Calling on the Higher Self, we increase the accuracy and intensity to such a point that we have a Laser beam. With the focus of the Middle Self and intensity of the Lower Self, the Higher Self has pinpoint focus.

This is a process. We may not be able to release all the limiting emotions all at once, but we CAN foster a habit of releasing them more easily, quickly and lovingly each time they arise. We can then replace those limitations with positive feelings and memories. Having "focused clearly" by journaling, we affirm positive thoughts. "Breathing deeply" to intentionally focus and build up our energy, we imagine positive events, experience them, and then access them as memory. "Believing completely", we affirm the reality of what we wish to accomplish, and then send that energized affirmation on to the Higher Self to be manifested within the environment.

With a completed affirmation (at least for the present), one that feels comfortable, like it will accomplish your needs and wants, you can work with it and empower it. On the way to sleep, and upon arising, center and relax. Put yourself into a receptive and relaxed state. Breathe slowly and deeply, using the Yogic Breath.

On one of the outbreaths, state the affirmation aloud or mentally. Take another breath, and on the outbreath, state the affirmation again, continuing until you have stated it ten times. Counting them out on your fingers is an easy way to stay on track. If you fall asleep before completing the affirmation ten times, that's great! Reprogramming the Lower Self is of importance here, not the strict adherence to ritual.

While repeating the affirmation, generate supportive feelings. Keep in mind, from memory or imagination, a situation that reflects the positive thoughts. Even if you can only remember one positive experience, replay that one over and over.

If you can't remember a positive experience, MAKE ONE UP!

During this time, do not focus on any negative responses. This is a time to generate only positive thoughts and feelings. There's plenty of time later to journal about any resistance you may have. NOT NOW!

While stating the affirmation with each outbreath and recalling supportive "memories", you can also focus on some tangible goals. Keep the affirmation short and sweet and to the point. Use a "meta"-physical affirmation, but with any number of specific visualizations to manifest exactly what you wish. Involving your senses more deeply, you can visualize another person (a loved one or authority figure), saying the affirmation to you. With all the senses in play, get totally involved with the process of changing the environment.

When trying to change the old tapes and manifest more positive thoughts, I recommend writing the affirmation on a piece of paper. Hang it in places where you can see it easily, places you cannot avoid throughout the day (eg. on the wall across from the toilet, the refrigerator door, the daily calendar, the dashboard of your car). Be creative. Be flexible. Cement the affirmation, relaxation and healing energies firmly in your mind, body and heart.

By working with memories, feelings and thoughts in this form, we focus upon that part of ourselves that already has or has had what we need and want. We allow it to grow and tangibly manifest. Through affirmations we HEAR what we want. Through imagery we SEE what we want. Using the breath, we energize ourselves and FEEL the thoughts and pictures. Empowering our healthy memories, thoughts, pictures and feelings, we can now manifest a more positive life.

- - -

Creating Our Reality

The process of self-discovery and mastery is diverse. No one can really take a wrong turn. Even the tangents and side-trips always have lessons. We can learn as much from the hinderers as we can from the helpers. We continually learn, change, and grow toward the Light.

By breathing and focusing our intent upon alternative, non-ordinary, or inner realities, we can let go of the Middle Self's focus, releasing our expectations of the way we think things "should" be. Learning to communicate with the different parts of our psyche, we access the Lower and Higher Selves, and change the way we view the world. We learn to journey through non-ordinary reality and the world of Spirit, integrating those realities in order to have a fuller experience and existence within this thing we call life.

Learning to Ground, to return to what is comfortable and explainable, it becomes safe to explore the unknown and work within other realities. With Guidance, we focus upon the proper goals, learning lessons with power and love on all levels. We explore what it means to manifest what we need and want in ways that are for the

Highest Good of ourselves and all concerned. Recognizing that life is a process, we explore our personal belief systems and change them!

Interpreting the environment symbolically, we discover our own unique personal mythologies. We discover what "personal laws" or "core beliefs" may be helping or hindering us on our journey. Uncovering the hindrances, we then decide which positive thought and limitless affirmation we would like to see manifest.

Being human, we give ourselves permission to have limitations and are more aware of them when they arise. Through self-talk, we discover the resistance and release it, empowering our selves and our thoughts. Remembering to ground, affirming the Highest Good, burning some Karma, sending the White Heart and Unconditional Love to others, we empower not only ourselves, but others as well.

Using the breath, personal symbology, feeling, seeing, hearing and being limitless, we become one with the positive, and we manifest that within the environment. We heal ourselves, others and everything around us.

Manifest!

Sit comfortably with your back straight and your hips higher than your knees, allowing power to run freely up the spine.

Have a goal and a specific affirmation seated firmly in your mind. Breathe deeply, all the way down to the abdomen. Repeat the goal and affirmation. Breathe Spirit, the White Light, down to the tailbone, the survival center. Remember the goal and any other goals related to the affirmation. See any associated symbols and desired consequences.

Take ten "connected" breaths--do not hesitate at all between inhaling and exhaling. Focus on the affirmation, the goal, the symbols. Let the energy and Light build up within your tailbone area. Breathe deep and hold it. Build up the energy emotionally, physically, and Spiritually. Feel the unlimited power of the universe as you vigorously affirm:

I Deserve It! * I Have The Right To It! * I've Worked Hard Enough For It! * I've Waited Long Enough For It! * I Can Have It! * I Want It! * I Am Willing To Have It! * I'm Ready For It! * I Accept It! * I Deserve It...

Let the energy, thoughts, feelings and symbols build up deep within you. Then, release the breath, shooting the energy and Light up the spine and out the top of the head. Like a fountain, it erupts, surrounding you with Love, Light and Power. Energy abounds as the fountain expands. It expends endlessly, surrounding the Earth and all its inhabitants. The thoughts and feelings are now manifesting. There is nothing that can stand in the way of that Love and Light, nothing at all!

So Be It!

You have just sent out to the universe a creative thought filled with life and energy. Your manifestation will come back to you, making tangible that which you have affirmed. Pay attention! Thank yourself, bless life, appreciate the beauty and wisdom of Spirit.

You may get exactly what you anticipated in exactly the form you wished for. Or, you may experience some surprises, some reflections of additional kinks in the hose, some areas begging for further clarification. All is perfect, and you now have the tools and awareness to begin the process anew.

Life, after all, is about HOW we experience, respond to, and interact with the world. There is no beginning and no end–there is only the choice of how to "be" in the world in the present moment. May this moment be one of expanding awareness, self-acceptance, limitless response-ability, and infinite Love.

- - -

Appendices

Appendix I: Colors: Commonly Accepted Interpretations

Many colors have both a positive aspect and a limiting aspect. When looking at a color, if it is bright or feels good and freeing, then we can assume a positive aspect. If, however, the color is dark or dull, if it is limiting or restrictive in feeling or breath, then we can assume a limiting aspect. The interpretations of these colors are meant only as a general guide and do not need to be adhered to strictly. If you follow interpretations that differ from mine, then I encourage you to hold on to your viewpoint.

Violet: Many people with strong religious convictions surround themselves with this color. However, if the religious beliefs contain limiting judgements and/or anger, the color will contain both the positive AND limiting aspects.
  Positive Aspect: certainty and faith
  Limiting Aspect: stubbornness and dogma
Lavender:
  Positive Aspect: gentleness, broad perspective
  Limiting Aspect: lack of assertiveness
Blue:
  Positive Aspect: peacefulness, a state of meditation
  Limiting Aspect: laziness
Green: Jealousy and envy are not necessarily limiting–these feelings let us know what it is that WE want. They are limiting if they lead us to possessiveness - wishing to have what someone else has at his or her expense.
  Positive Aspect: growth, healing, patience, a gradual process
  Limiting Aspect: jealous or envious of others' positive aspects
Yellow:
  Positive Aspect: mental activity, intellect, thoughtfulness, planning
  Limiting Aspect: procrastination, lack of physical and/or emotional activity

Red: Red, like violet, must often be taken in context with feelings and visual cues in order to know whether it reflects a positive or limiting aspect. Red accompanied by a warm, sensual feeling may indicate nurturing. If the feeling, however, is heavy or "dark", then we can assume anger and limitations.

Positive Aspect: activity; physical, emotional and/or Spiritual

Limiting Aspect: anger, hyperactivity, lack of thought, an overinvestment in the physical realities

Orange: Orange implies process, movement, balance and change.

Positive Aspect: thought (Yellow) backed up by physical or emotional activity (Red), planning and activity (Red) followed by thought (Yellow), reviewing one's actions

Limiting Aspect: lack of acceptance, needing change

White:

Positive Aspect: Spiritual energies, creativity, love, that which is beyond physical reality

Limiting Aspect: None

Black:

Positive Aspect: transformation, inevitable change, moving on to a Higher plane of reality, death of a way of being (not necessarily a physical death)

Limiting Aspect: painful transformation, resistance to completely letting go of a limiting situation, not necessarily a physical death

Gold:

Positive Aspect: cleansing of thought and belief leading to experience and wisdom

Limiting Aspect: none

Pink:

Positive Aspect: unconditional love (White) actively expressed (Red), Spiritual healing (combining Spiritual and physical realities)

Limiting Aspect: none

Brown:

Positive Aspect: grounding, connection with the Earth

Limiting Aspect: lack of mental, emotional or Spiritual energies, possibly "stuck in the mud"

Gray:

Positive Aspect: transition, freedom of thought, connecting with Spirit, movement between realities

Limiting Aspect: stagnation, "lost in the fog"

- - -

Appendix II: Numbers: Interpretations and Affirmations

There are many treatises on Numerology, some of which agree with this one, and some of which differ. If you already have a numerical system that works for you, feel free to stick with that system. Each number or set of numbers may be reduced down to a one or two digit number. For example: 53 = (5 + 3) = 8
765 = (7 + 6 + 5) = 18 = (1 + 8) = 9
4,731 = (4 + 7 + 3 + 1) = 15 = (1 + 5) = 6
677 = (6 + 7 + 7) = 20 = (2 + 0) = 2

We always reduce numbers to a single digit (1 through 9), with the following exceptions. (a) The number 12 may be expressed as 12/3 because there is a separate meaning for both the 12 and the 3 (see explanation below). (b) Multiples of 11 are considered to be "master numbers" with a lot of power. They have meanings of their own, but may also be reduced to a single digit. For example: 11 = 11/2, 22 = 22/4, 33 = 33/6, 44 = 44/8 and so on.

As you look at the numbers below, take a second to see if there is a number that has a specific meaning in your own life. Each number below has a challenge or lesson attached to it. There are no limitations except how we choose to meet those challenges and learn the lessons.

1 - New Beginnings, New Ideas, New Relationships, Leadership, Planting Seeds for the Future

Challenge: Completion vs. Beginning Anew, Loneliness vs. Cooperation
Affirmation: I safely act on my decisions and my feelings at the perfect time and with the perfect support.

The person under this energy may (often unjustly) be accused of snobbishness because of aloofness and the need to be in charge. The # 1 often undergoes change faster than others and needs to be aware of wrongly judging others for not changing fast enough. Things always get finished at the perfect time, not necessarily on a prearranged schedule.

2 - Partnerships, Associations, Cooperation, Identity

Challenge: Within a Relationship - Keeping vs. Losing One's Identity.
Affirmation: I safely share my independence with others. I allow others to share their independence with me.

The challenge here is two-fold: (1) how to keep one's own identity and individuality within a relationship and (2) how to challenge another person to keep his or her own identity and uniqueness.

3 - Communications, Self Expression, Creativity

Challenge: Listening to the Inner Voice vs. Expressing oneself Outwardly, Expressing Creativity While Alone or in the Presence of Others

Affirmation: I safely acknowledge my feelings. I express myself at the perfect time and in the perfect form.

The # 3 needs to know when it is time to focus on communicating with oneself, and when it is time to communicate with others.

4 - Organization, Productivity, Stability

Challenge: Planning and Surety Regarding the Future vs. Spontaneity and Taking a Leap of Faith

Affirmation: I have the perfect understanding at the perfect time, and I act on my decisions at the perfect time.

If out of balance, the # 4 can have an overinvestment in understanding things rather than accepting them.

5 - Change and Willingness to Change

Challenge: Flexibility and Change vs. Stubbornness and Stagnation

Affirmation: All my changes are for the Highest Good of my self and all concerned, and I allow others to support me on this (and I attract the perfect support for this).

The # 5 can be the true social butterfly–the Changeling or Chameleon with the ability to change colors with its surroundings. He must make sure he doesn't compromise with and conform too much to others, possibly losing sight of his own needs, wants and certainty.

6 - Service and Response-Ability

Challenge: Being Response-Able To Others While Serving the Self. Being Response-Able to Self While Serving Others.

Affirmation: I have the perfect level of response-ability at all times. I allow others to support me on my needs and wants. I allow myself to support others on their needs and wants.

Win/win situations are ALWAYS possible. Being response-able TO others does not mean being response-able FOR them.

7 - The Psychic, Introspection, Self-Analysis

Challenge: Thought vs. Action

Affirmation: My sensitivity is one of my strengths. I act on my feelings and my decisions at the perfect time and in the perfect form.

If out of balance, the # 7 can find himself spending much time in lonely introspection or much time with others in order to avoid introspection. Structured time with others may balance this. The # 7 may also need to take things at face value, rather than taking things too personally.

8 - Successful Activity on the Earth Plane
Challenge: Security vs. Risk
Affirmation: I am at the perfect place, at the perfect time, with the perfect people, successfully engaged in the perfect activity.

When balancing security and risk in one's life, things can fall in to place "as if by magic". However, when out of balance, things can fall apart just as creatively.

9 - Completion AND Compassion
Challenge: Blame vs. Forgiveness, Holding On vs. Letting Go
Affirmation: I allow others to feel safe with my feelings. I can feel safe with others' feelings. I act on my feelings at the perfect time.

We must be in a state of completion with ourselves and others. This does not mean ending relationships but rather, knowing when it is time to jump out of a sinking ship, and when it is time to keep it afloat. The # 9 can learn to be honest AND compassionate at the same time, owning his feelings without blaming himself and/or others. Lists of unfinished business and incomplete communications may be useful.

- - -

The numbers, 11/2, 12/3, 22/4, 33/6 and 44/8 are called master numbers, with dual meanings and lessons. They are very powerful and usually appear when we have something important to learn or to act on. The lowest digit (eg. # 2) expresses itself through the larger number (eg. # 11).

11/2 - The Master Magician,
Expressing One's Independence in a Relationship
Challenge: Going Through Obstacles or Around them., Use of Power vs. Abuse of Power
Affirmation: I safely use my power with Love, and I express my Love with power. I allow others to do the same.

The # 11 may have a tendency to grow up in an abusive and/or neglectful family setting. He may also attract an extraordinary amount of illness and/or dis-ease in order to challenge and hone his personal power.

12/3 - Self Expression through Change, The Rebirth
Challenge: Going Through Changes Fast vs. Slow
Affirmation: I continually acknowledge that all my changes are for the Highest Good. I safely and easily experience the joy in my life.

The # 12 has the tendency to make SWEEPING changes in life all at once, and may need to remember moderation and temperance.

22/4 - Stability Within Relationships
Challenge: Stagnancy vs. Growth
Affirmation: I affirm the perfect order of the Universe. I affirm the uniqueness and perfection of myself and all those around me. I am always in the perfect relationships.

33/6 - Service Through Communication
Challenge: Service Through Communication vs. Communication Through Service
Affirmation: I safely communicate with others honestly, response-ably and lovingly. And I allow others to do the same.

44/8 - Successful Action Through Planning
Challenge: Planning Ahead or Reviewing One's Actions vs. Taking Action. Past & Future vs. Present
Affirmation: I safely plan for the future, complete the past, and express myself in the present.

The 55, 66, 77, 88 and 99 are also master numbers, but are not as powerful as the ones previously discussed.

- # 55/10/1   Leadership Through the ability to Change
- # 66/12/3   Communication and Change Through Service
- # 77/14/5   Change Through Inner Exploration
- # 88/16/7   Inner Exploration Through Tangible Expression on the Earth
- # 99/18/9   Feeling Complete Through Helping Others to Feel Complete, Forgiving Others Through Helping Others to Forgive

- - -

Footnotes

Chapter 2
1. Serge Kahili King, Ph.D., Urban Shaman, A Handbook For Personal And Planetary Transformation Based On The Hawaiian Way Of The Adventurer, (New York, NY: Fireside/Simon & Schuster, Inc., 1990), p.14.
2. Ibid, p.22
3. Ibid, p.22
4. Sandra Ingerman, The Shamanic Journey, Power And Healing, Foundation For Shamanic Studies, workshop (Colorado Spg., CO, 1991).
5. King, Urban Shaman, p.36
6. Maxwell Freedom Long, The Secret Science Behind Miracles, (Marina Del Rey, CA: Devorss & Co. Publishers, 14th Printing, 1982).
7. Enid Hoffman, Huna, A Beginner's Guide, (Rockport, MA: Para Research, Inc., 1976), p.94.

Chapter 3
8. Edith Hamilton, Mythology, Timeless Tales Of Gods And Heroes, (New York, NY: Mentor Books, New American Library, Inc., 1942), pp. 92-100.
9. Joan Halifax, Ph.D., Shamanic Voices, A Survey Of Visionary Narratives, (New York, NY: E.P. Dutton, 1979), p.28.

Chapter 4
10. James Stewart, Ph.D., workshop on Mythology, Fairytales And The Craft Of Healing, (Boulder, CO, 1979).
11. David B. Guralnik, General Editor, Webster's New World Dictionary, Concise Edition, (Cleveland, OH & New York, NY: World Publishing Co., 1964), p.862.
12. Yogi Ramacharaka, Science Of Breath, (Chicago, IL: Yogi Publication Society, 1904), pp.37-42.

Chapter 5
13. King, Urban Shaman, p.15.

Chapter 6
14. Enid Hoffman, Huna, A Beginner's Guide, p.93.
15. King, Urban Shaman, p.136.
16. Ibid, p.144.
17. Ibid, p.140.

18. Michael Harner, The Way Of The Shaman, (New York, NY, Toronto, Canada: Bantam Books, 1982/Harper & Row Publishers, Inc., 1980), p.90.
19. King, Urban Shaman, p.140, p.144.
20. Harner, The Way Of The Shaman, pp.30-38.
21. King, Urban Shaman, p.144.
22. Serge King, Kahuna Healing, (Wheaton, IL: Theosophical Publishing House, 1983), p.53.

Chapter 7
23. Dr. Duran, Trance Channeling by Trina Kamp, Scottsdale, AZ, (Denver, CO, 1979).
24. Don Meichenbaum, Ph.D., workshop on Cognitive Behavior Modification, (Denver, CO: Evaluation Research Association, Inc., 1985).

Chapter 8
25. Serge King, Urban Shaman, pp.124-135.
26. Sondra Ray, Loving Relationships, (Berkeley, CA: Celestial Art, 1980), p.66.

Chapter 9
27. Enid Hoffman, Huna, A Beginner's Guide, p.35.
28. Ibid, p.17.
29. Albert Ellis, Colorado Association For Counseling And Guidance Annual Conference, (Colorado Spg., CO, 1985).

Chapter 11
30. Maxwell Freedom Long, Self-Suggestion, (Marina Del Rey, CA: Devorss & CO. Publishers, 1958), p.73.
31. Sondra Ray, Loving Relationships, p.11.
32. Ibid, p.26.

Chapter 13
33. Virginia Hooven, Kahuna Healing Workshop, (Boulder, CO, 1980).
34. Taisha Abelar, The Sorcerer's Crossing, A Woman's Journey, (New York, NY: Penguin Books/Arkana, 1992).
35. Francine Shapiro, Eye Movement Desensitization & Reprocessing; Basic Principles, Protocols And Procedures, (New York, NY: Guilford Pres, 1995).

Chapter 14
36. Richard Bandler and John Grinder, Frogs Into Princes: Neuro Linguistic Programming, (Moab, UT: Real People Press, 1979).

- - -

Bibliography & Additional Reading
(those not listed in Footnotes)

- O. Carl Simonton, M.D., Stephanie Matthews-Simonton & James L. Creighton, Getting Well Again, (United States & Canada: Bantam Books, 1980).
- Serge King, Imagineering For Health, (Illinois, USA: Theosophical Publishing House, A Quest Book, 1981). Mastering Your Hidden Self, (Ibid, 1985).
- Louise L. Hay, You Can Heal Your Life, (California, USA: Hay House, Inc., 1984).
- Maxwell Freedom Long, Growing Into Light, (California, USA: Huna Research Publications, 1955).
- L. Ron Hubbard, Dianetics, The Modern Science Of Mental Health, (California, USA: Church Of Scientology, 1950).
- Carlos Castaneda, The Teachings Of Don Juan, (New York, NY, USA: Simon & Schuster, 1968). A Separate Reality, (Ibid, 1971). Journey To Ixtlan, (Ibid, 1972). Tales Of Power, (Ibid, 1974). The Second Ring Of Power, (Ibid, 1977).
- Gerald Jampolsky, Love Is Letting Go Of Fear, (California, USA: Celestial Arts, 1979).

- - -

About The Author

Inspired by a personal search for healing that took him through Buddhist and Hindu disciplines, multi-cultural Shamanic traditions, and metaphysical studies, Steven Rogat brings a powerful and uniquely versatile perspective to his work.

As a professional counselor and intuitive healer, he is adept at integrating the physical, emotional and spiritual dimensions of health, generating new possibilities for wellness. When he is not meeting with clients, teaching a seminar, producing a radio show, lecturing or writing, he may be found fly fishing a lazy river or hiking the woods with his family.

- - -

You can contact the author at email: rogat@usa.net. Copies of this book are available at your local bookstore, or by sending name & address (print clearly) with $11.95 (includes tax), plus $4.00 shipping & handling, (U.S. currency) in check or money order payable to:

Creative Thought Press
P.O. Box 2791
Chapel Hill, NC 27515

- - -

Other Books By Steven Rogat

Spirit Journeys: Freeing the Soul in this Life and Beyond, co-written with Marcia Rogat. In print - August, 2002.
The Body as Symbol: Healing Through Positive Thought, soon to be in print, title may change due to publisher's preference.